HORSING AROUND

JOURNAL AND ACTIVITY BOOK

LEXI REES

Published in Great Britain
By Outset Publishing Ltd

First edition published November 2021

Written by Lexi Rees

Design by FountainCreative.co.uk
Illustrations from Shutterstock.com and iStock.com

Copyright © Lexi Rees 2021

Lexi Rees has asserted their rights under the Copyright, Designs and Patents Act 1988 to be identified as the author of this work.

All rights reserved. No part of this publication may be reproduced, stored in a retrieval system, or transmitted, in any form or by any means, without the prior permission in writing of the publisher, nor be otherwise circulated in any form of binding or cover other than that in which it is published and without a similar condition including this condition being imposed on the subsequent purchaser.

ISBN 978-1-913799-07-6

This journal belongs to

_____

_____

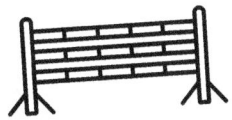
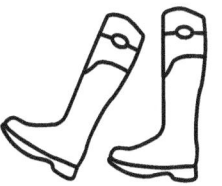

MONTH: ....

My riding goals

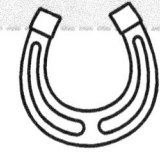
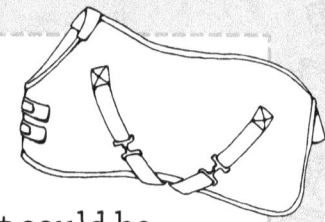

What would you like to do better or learn? For example, it could be to keep your heels down, develop a deeper seat, master the half halt, improve your jumping, ride a perfect leg yield, or maybe even try a *piaffe*.

Make a list of the things you want to focus on this month. If you're not sure what to pick, ask your instructor.

Goal 1: _____

_____

_____

Goal 2: _____

_____

_____

Goal 3: _____

_____

_____

I ....

do hereby commit to practising these things every time I ride.

Signed: ....

Date: ....

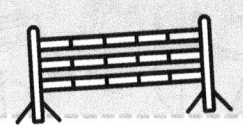

Using a goal tracker can help you achieve your targets.

GOAL	Colour in a horseshoe every time you practise
1	
2	
3	

Write or draw your goals!

WEEK ONE

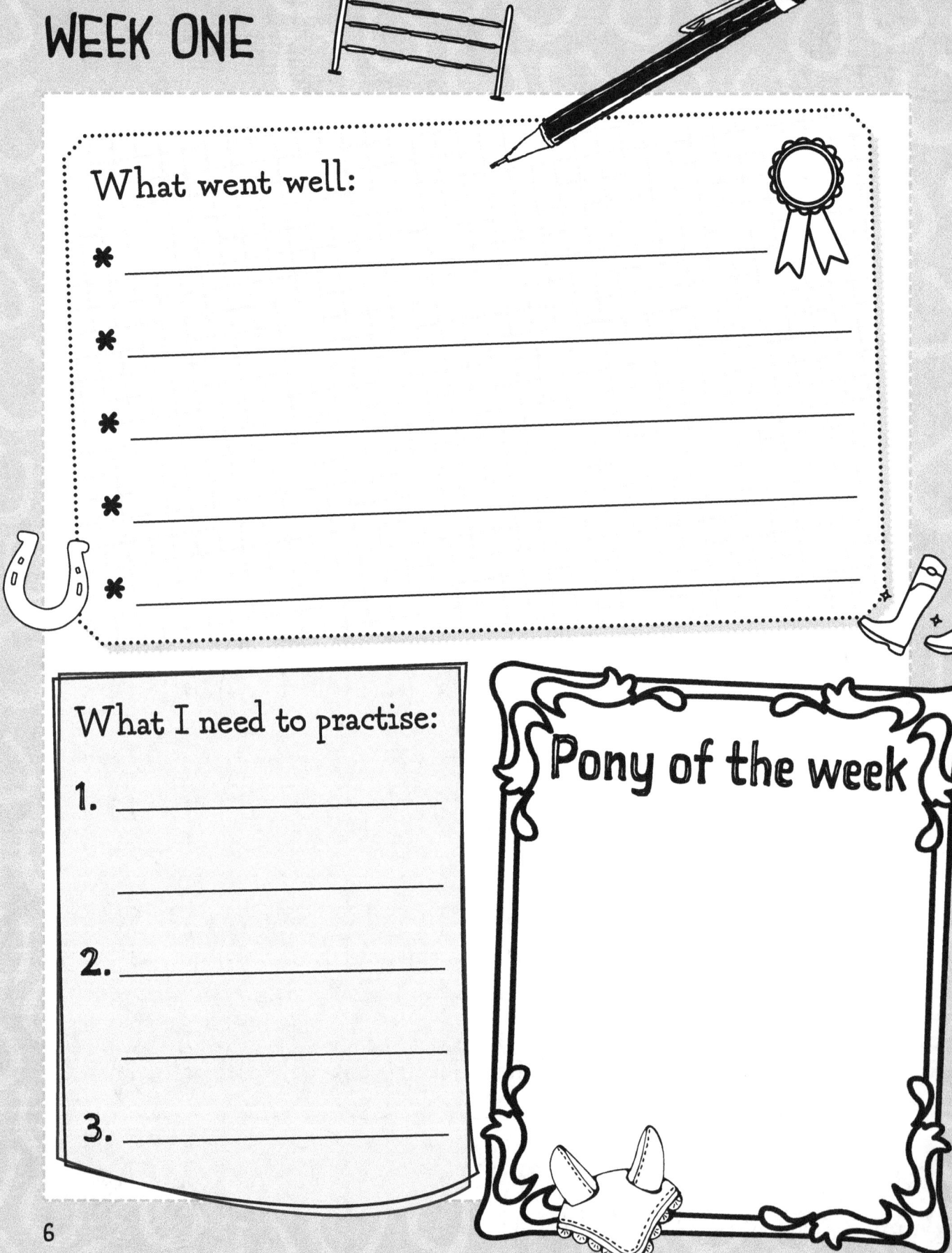

What went well:

* _____
* _____
* _____
* _____
* _____

What I need to practise:

1. _____

2. _____

3. _____

Pony of the week

THIS WEEK I HAVE ...

- ○ Groomed
- ○ Cleaned tack
- ○ Mucked out
- ○ Had a lesson
- ○ Helped with feeding
- ○ Been for a hack
- ○ Learnt something new
- ○ Ridden a different pony

MY LESSON TRACKER

Name: _____

Age: _____

○ Mare

○ Gelding

Q: What disease are horses scared of?
A: Hay fever!

WEEK TWO

What went well:

* _____
* _____
* _____
* _____
* _____

What I need to practise:

1. _____

2. _____

3. _____

Pony of the week

THIS WEEK I HAVE ...

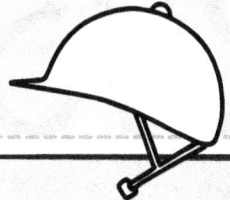

- ○ Groomed
- ○ Cleaned tack
- ○ Mucked out
- ○ Had a lesson
- ○ Helped with feeding
- ○ Been for a hack
- ○ Learnt something new
- ○ Ridden a different pony

MY LESSON TRACKER

Name: _____

Age: _____

○ Mare

○ Gelding

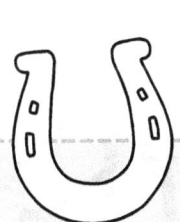

THIS WEEK I HAVE ...

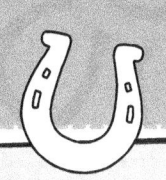

- ○ Groomed
- ○ Cleaned tack
- ○ Mucked out
- ○ Had a lesson
- ○ Helped with feeding
- ○ Been for a hack
- ○ Learnt something new
- ○ Ridden a different pony

MY LESSON TRACKER

Name: _____

Age: _____

○ Mare

○ Gelding

According to legend ...

A horse found in the morning with a tangled and twisted mane and tail has been ridden by pixies.

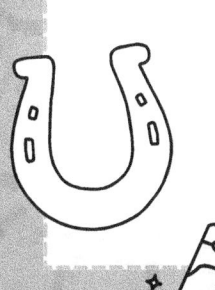

WEEK FOUR

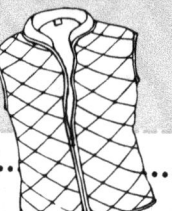

What went well:

* _____
* _____
* _____
* _____
* _____

What I need to practise:

1. _____
   _____
2. _____
   _____
3. _____

Pony of the week

THIS WEEK I HAVE ...

- ○ Groomed
- ○ Cleaned tack
- ○ Mucked out
- ○ Had a lesson
- ○ Helped with feeding
- ○ Been for a hack
- ○ Learnt something new
- ○ Ridden a different pony

MY LESSON TRACKER

Name: _____

Age: _____

- ○ Mare
- ○ Gelding

TACK UP

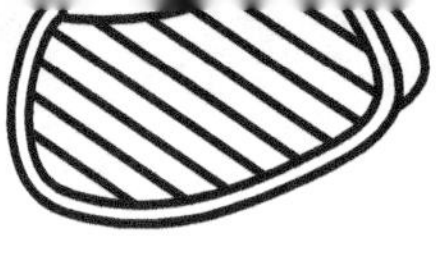

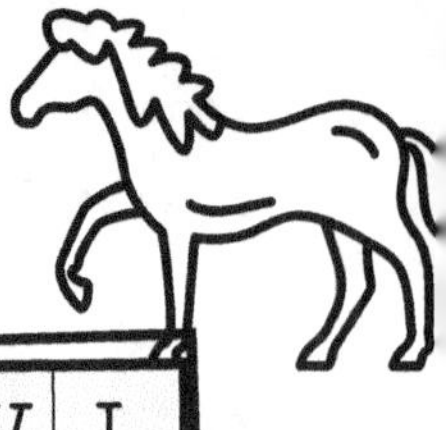

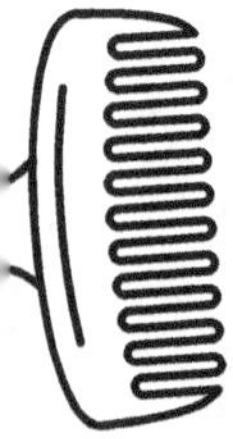

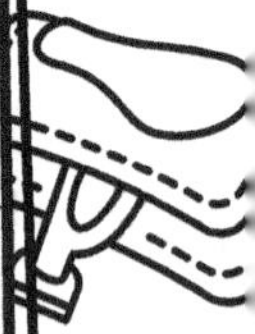

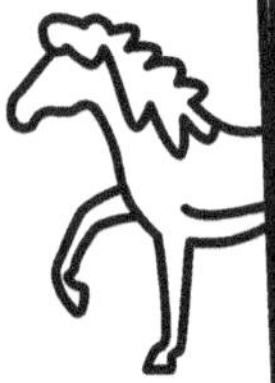

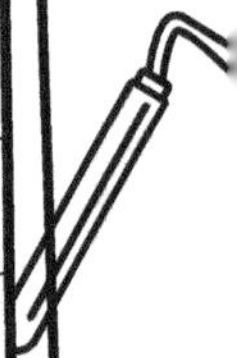

I	L	T	N	G	I	R	T	J	E	O	S	V	T	P	W	W	L
F	P	D	L	B	R	Y	E	L	T	T	X	T	A	L	W	H	Q
B	V	A	V	I	P	O	A	T	I	E	K	A	C	Q	A	V	F
P	O	L	L	A	G	G	O	R	N	T	N	Q	K	P	U	H	F
F	F	I	W	X	N	M	R	M	R	A	O	D	R	O	P	J	K
R	L	K	Z	I	J	U	K	O	I	V	C	G	O	Q	J	P	H
N	Y	Z	T	F	P	C	T	R	E	N	N	W	O	X	J	F	J
R	U	R	S	C	H	O	O	L	I	N	G	M	M	Z	Z	H	E
P	A	M	B	T	A	E	D	D	S	T	A	B	L	E	M	H	L
M	J	S	N	M	M	I	I	O	C	G	I	L	T	B	Z	R	D
P	I	J	K	A	R	X	Z	O	N	V	S	U	E	J	J	E	D
T	Y	F	S	B	H	R	E	H	I	M	Y	N	T	V	T	F	A
I	D	N	G	D	C	Q	D	E	Q	V	B	G	X	U	I	T	S
B	K	Z	X	B	W	U	N	K	I	U	E	E	N	E	H	Z	M
E	X	U	L	G	U	W	F	L	X	D	Y	B	J	I	P	O	Z
I	I	O	M	L	I	U	Q	X	C	K	N	E	O	S	W	J	G
Z	K	A	T	G	P	Y	T	I	K	Q	T	N	Q	Y	F	E	Q
Z	X	W	L	F	L	N	S	Y	E	C	H	U	C	K	L	A	W

BIT
BRIDLE
CANTER
GALLOP
GROOMING
HALT
LUNGE
MARTINGALE
NUMNAH
SADDLE
SCHOOLING
STABLE
STIRRUP
TACKROOM
TROT
WALK

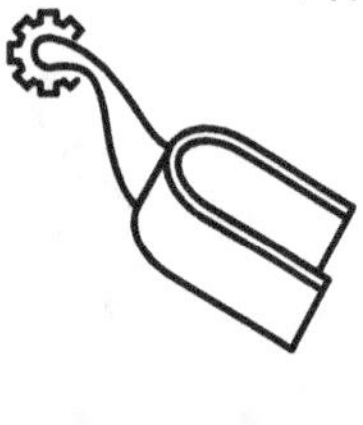

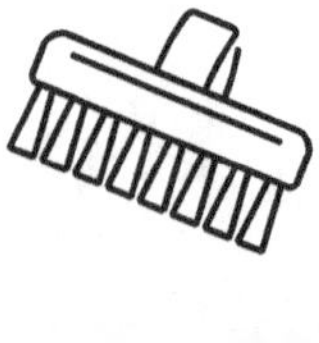

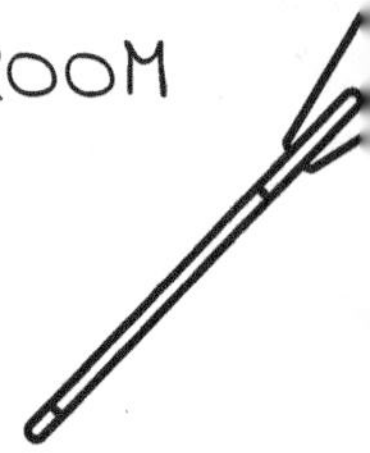

Answers on page 172

HORSE BREED ANAGRAMS

Can you unscramble the letters to find the different horse breeds?

ATDESHLN   _ _ _ _ _ _ _ _ _

BARNAAI   _ _ _ _ _ _ _

ATSMUNG   _ _ _ _ _ _ _

HRSIE   _ _ _ _ _

ORFJD   _ _ _ _ _

SNOUALIT   _ _ _ _ _ _ _ _

ORRECHPEN   _ _ _ _ _ _ _ _ _

NAGMRO   _ _ _ _ _ _

GNIERFLHA   _ _ _ _ _ _ _ _ _

ASAOLOPPA   _ _ _ _ _ _ _ _ _

NAFIERSI   _ _ _ _ _ _ _ _

Answers on page 172

MONTH: ....

My riding goals

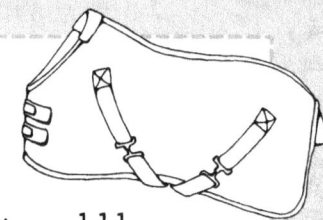

What would you like to do better or learn? For example, it could be to keep your heels down, develop a deeper seat, master the half halt, improve your jumping, ride a perfect leg yield, or maybe even try a *piaffe*.

Make a list of the things you want to focus on this month. If you're not sure what to pick, ask your instructor.

Goal 1: _____

_____

_____

Goal 2: _____

_____

_____

Goal 3: _____

_____

_____

I .... do hereby commit to practising these things every time I ride.

Signed: ....

Date: ....

18

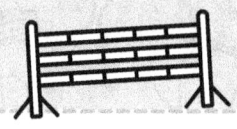

Using a goal tracker can help you achieve your targets.

GOAL	Colour in a horseshoe every time you practise
1	
2	
3	

Write or draw your goals!

WEEK ONE

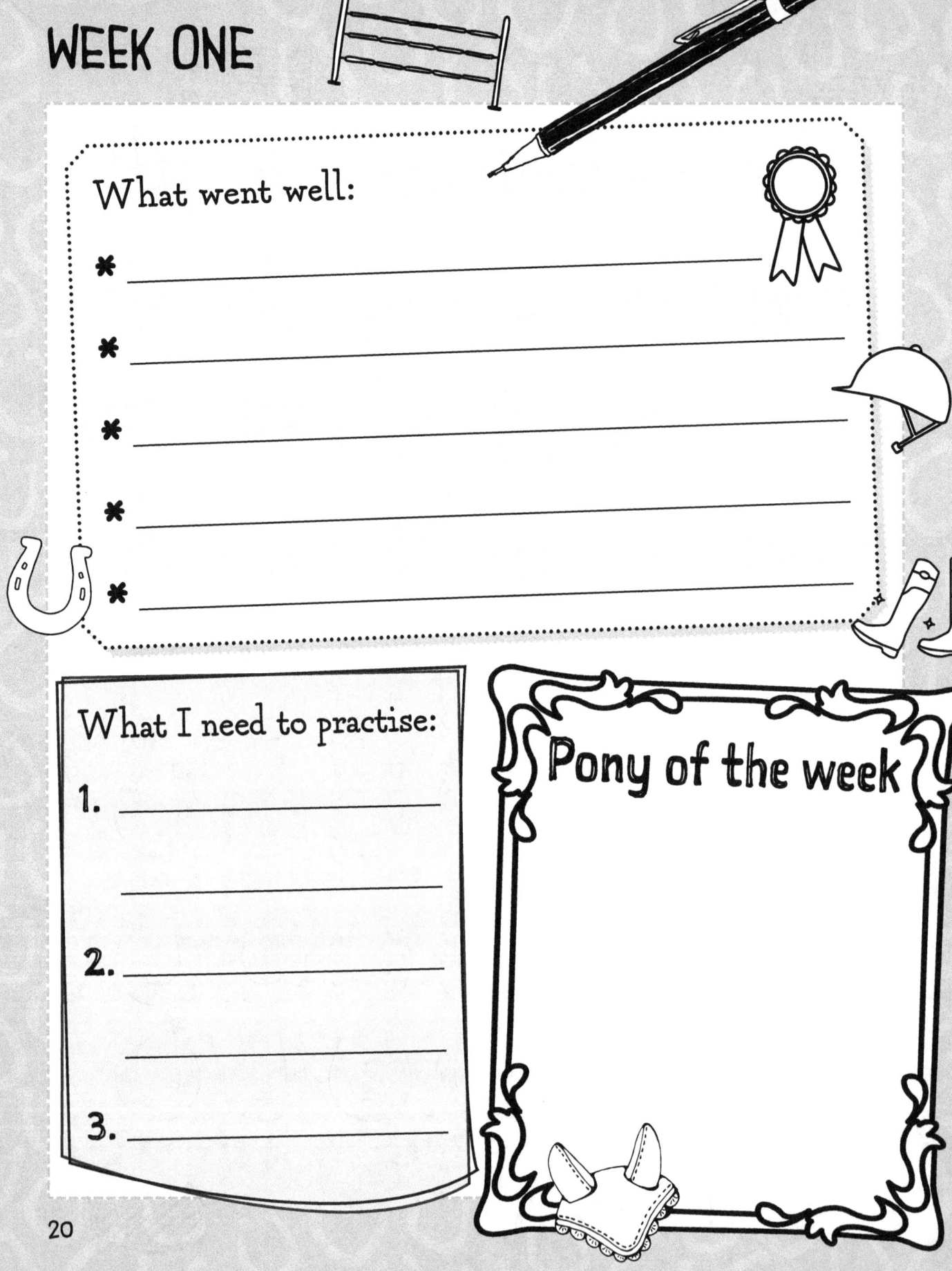

What went well:

* _____
* _____
* _____
* _____
* _____

What I need to practise:

1. _____
2. _____
3. _____

Pony of the week

THIS WEEK I HAVE ...

- ○ Groomed
- ○ Cleaned tack
- ○ Mucked out
- ○ Had a lesson
- ○ Helped with feeding
- ○ Been for a hack
- ○ Learnt something new
- ○ Ridden a different pony

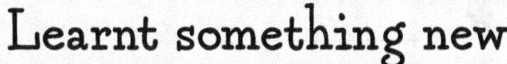

MY LESSON TRACKER

Name: _____

Age: _____

○ Mare

○ Gelding

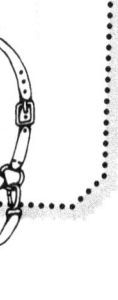

Q: What do you call a scary horse in the dark?
A: A night-mare!

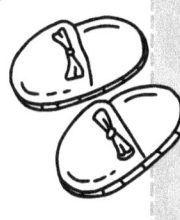
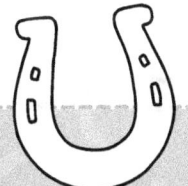

WEEK TWO

What went well:

* _____
* _____
* _____
* _____
* _____

What I need to practise:

1. _____
   _____
2. _____
   _____
3. _____

Pony of the week

THIS WEEK I HAVE ...

- ○ Groomed
- ○ Cleaned tack
- ○ Mucked out
- ○ Had a lesson
- ○ Helped with feeding
- ○ Been for a hack
- ○ Learnt something new
- ○ Ridden a different pony

MY LESSON TRACKER

Name: _____

Age: _____

○ Mare

○ Gelding

WEEK THREE

What went well:

* _____
* _____
* _____
* _____
* _____

What I need to practise:

1. _____
2. _____
3. _____

Pony of the week

THIS WEEK I HAVE ...

- ◯ Groomed
- ◯ Cleaned tack
- ◯ Mucked out
- ◯ Had a lesson
- ◯ Helped with feeding
- ◯ Been for a hack
- ◯ Learnt something new
- ◯ Ridden a different pony

MY LESSON TRACKER

Name: _____

Age: _____

◯ Mare

◯ Gelding

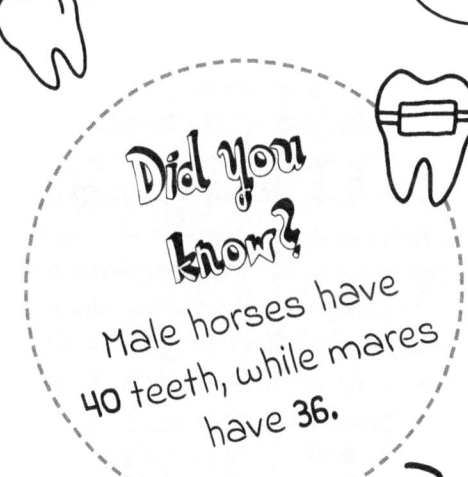

Did you know?

Male horses have **40** teeth, while mares have **36**.

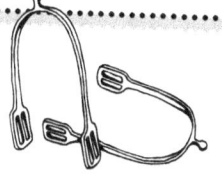

WEEK FOUR

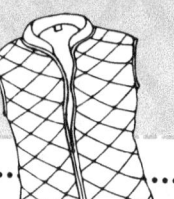

What went well:

* _____

* _____

* _____

* _____

* _____

What I need to practise:

1. _____

2. _____

3. _____

Pony of the week

THIS WEEK I HAVE ...

- ○ Groomed
- ○ Cleaned tack
- ○ Mucked out
- ○ Had a lesson
- ○ Helped with feeding
- ○ Been for a hack
- ○ Learnt something new
- ○ Ridden a different pony

MY LESSON TRACKER

Name: _____

Age: _____

- ○ Mare
- ○ Gelding

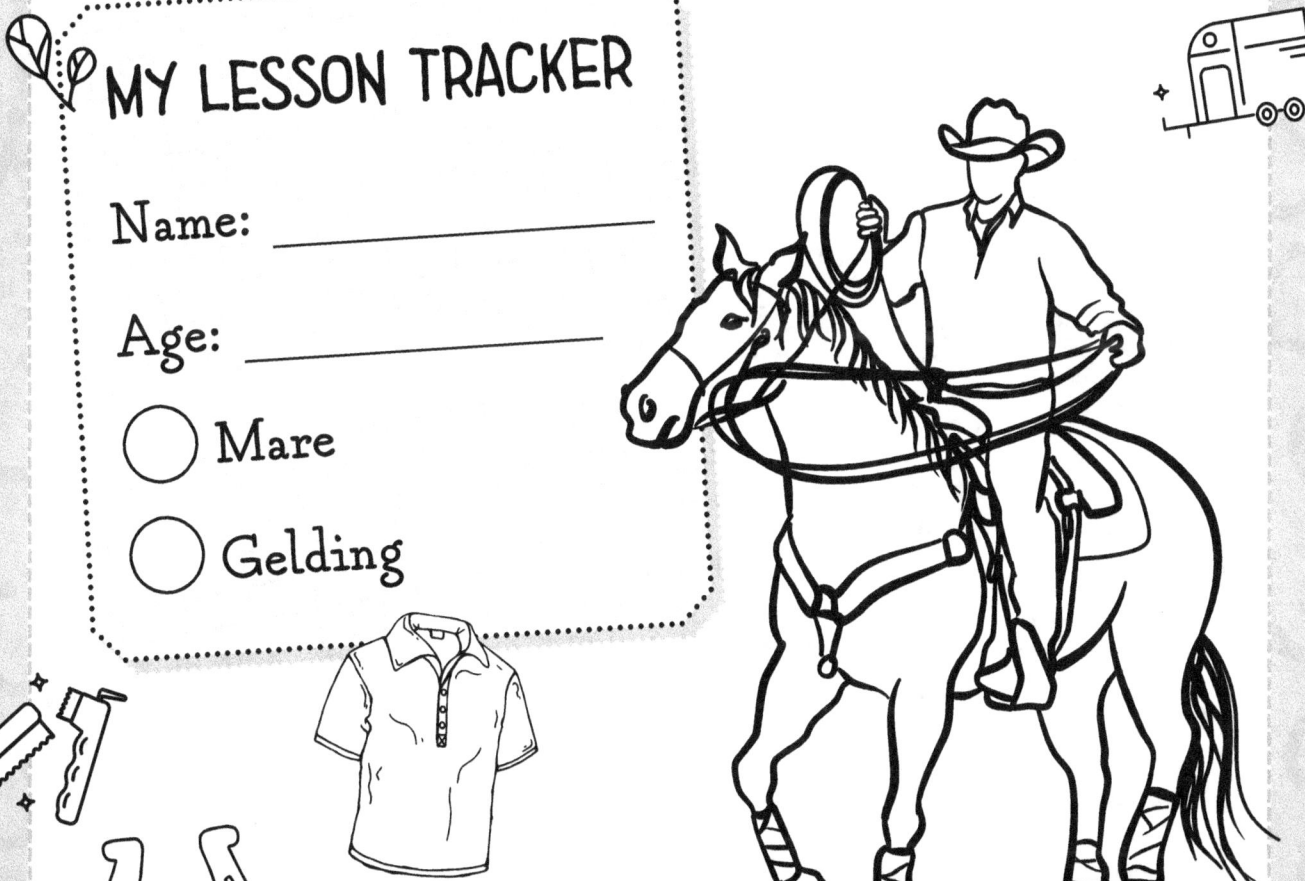

NAME THAT CLIP

Put the correct name for the clip under each drawing.

Hunter Chaser Bib
Blanket Full Strip
Trace Irish

Answers on page 172

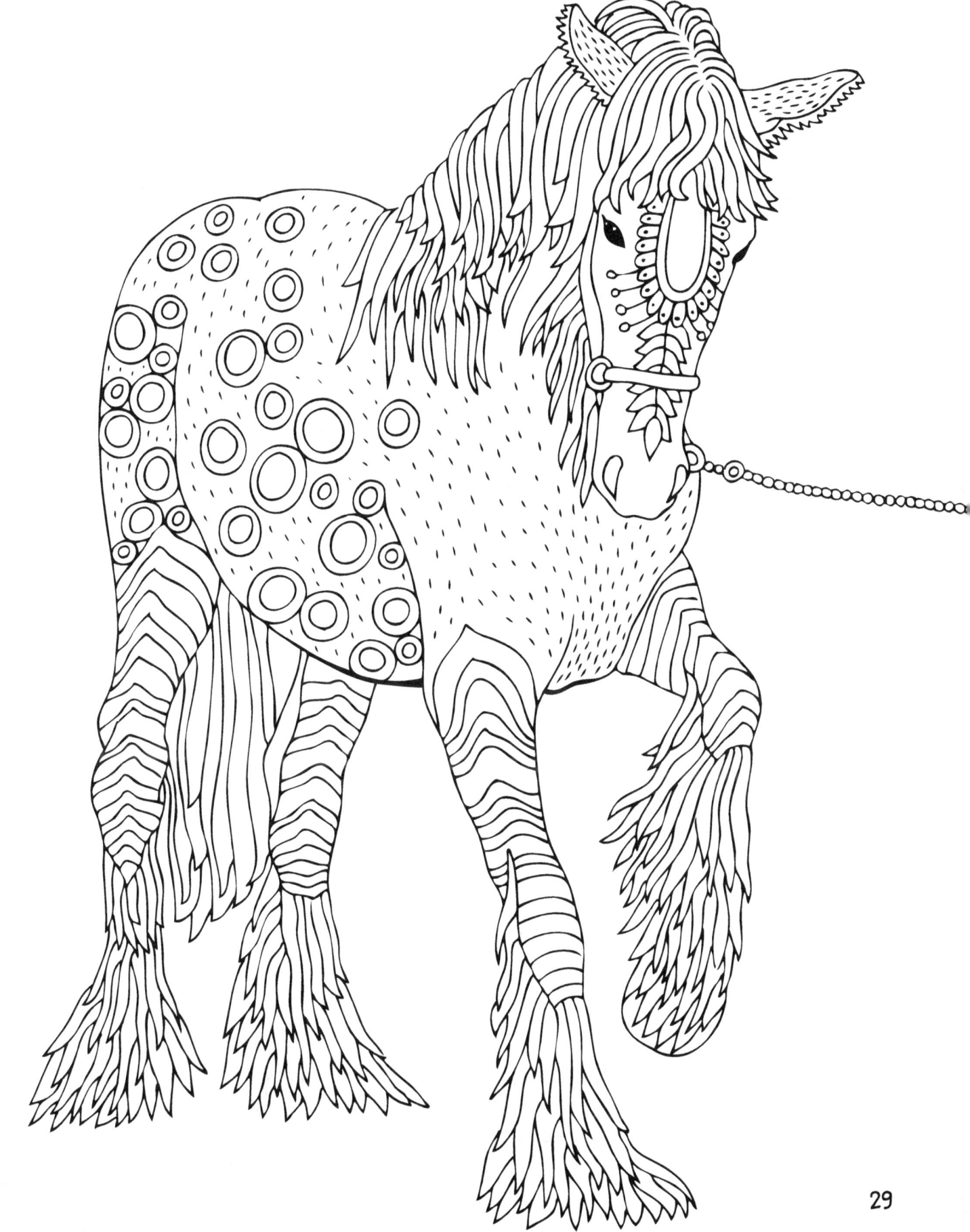

GLITTER HORSE

Make a sparkly horse for your desk.

You will need
* Two pieces of firm white card
* Colourful sequins or glitter
* Lots of pieces of embroidery thread or wool, cut to at least twice the desired length of the mane and tail (to give enough to plait or trim)
* Fine black marker pen
* Sticky tape
* Glue
* Two paperclips (to make it stand)
* Several clothes pegs to hold the horses together while the glue dries

1. Draw an outline of a horse on one piece of card. You can trace the outline on the next page if you like, or create your own.

2. Use this as a template and cut out another identical horse.

3. For the mane, take the shorter pieces of thread/wool, line then up along the wrong side (back) of one of the horse templates and stick them down with the tape.

4. Repeat with the longer thread for the tail.

5. Use the marker pen to draw the horse's face.

6. Cover the right side (front) of the horse in glue and decorate with sequins or glitter.

7. Repeat on the other horse outline. Note – you're going to stick the two shapes together, so make sure you don't confuse the right side/ wrong side!

8. Bend the paperclips in half and use tape to stick them to the wrong side (undecorated side) of both hind legs.

9. Glue the two horses together (this will hide the paperclips and the sticky tape) and carefully position the clothes pegs to hold it in place while it dries.

10. You can split each thread into strands to make the mane and tail fuller, or plait it if you prefer.

MONTH: ....

My riding goals

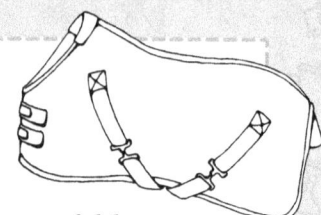

What would you like to do better or learn? For example, it could be to keep your heels down, develop a deeper seat, master the half halt, improve your jumping, ride a perfect leg yield, or maybe even try a *piaffe*.

Make a list of the things you want to focus on this month. If you're not sure what to pick, ask your instructor.

Goal 1: _____

_____

_____

Goal 2: _____

_____

_____

Goal 3: _____

_____

_____

I .... do hereby commit to practising these things every time I ride.

Signed: ....

Date: ....

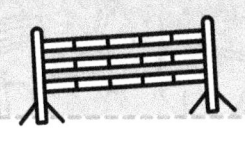

Using a goal tracker can help you achieve your targets.

GOAL	Colour in a horseshoe every time you practise
1	
2	
3	

Write or draw your goals!

WEEK ONE

What went well:

* _____
* _____
* _____
* _____
* _____

What I need to practise:

1. _____
_____

2. _____
_____

3. _____

Pony of the week

THIS WEEK I HAVE ...

- ○ Groomed
- ○ Cleaned tack
- ○ Mucked out
- ○ Had a lesson
- ○ Helped with feeding
- ○ Been for a hack
- ○ Learnt something new
- ○ Ridden a different pony

MY LESSON TRACKER

Name: _____

Age: _____

○ Mare

○ Gelding

Q: Where do horses go when they're sick?
A: The horsepital!

WEEK TWO

What went well:
* _____
* _____
* _____
* _____
* _____

What I need to practise:
1. _____
2. _____
3. _____

Pony of the week

THIS WEEK I HAVE ...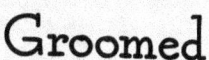

- ◯ Groomed
- ◯ Cleaned tack
- ◯ Mucked out
- ◯ Had a lesson
- ◯ Helped with feeding
- ◯ Been for a hack
- ◯ Learnt something new
- ◯ Ridden a different pony

MY LESSON TRACKER

Name: _____

Age: _____

- ◯ Mare
- ◯ Gelding

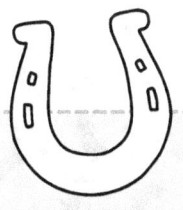
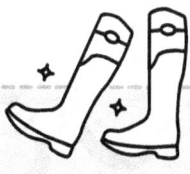

WEEK THREE

What went well:

* _____
* _____
* _____
* _____
* _____

What I need to practise:

1. _____
2. _____
3. _____

Pony of the week

THIS WEEK I HAVE ...

- ○ Groomed
- ○ Cleaned tack
- ○ Mucked out
- ○ Had a lesson
- ○ Helped with feeding
- ○ Been for a hack
- ○ Learnt something new
- ○ Ridden a different pony

MY LESSON TRACKER

Name: _____

Age: _____

○ Mare

○ Gelding

Did you know?

The hand size used to measure horses was standardised to 4 inches by King Henry VIII in 1514.

WEEK FOUR

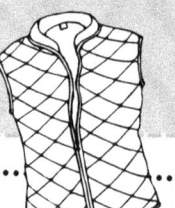
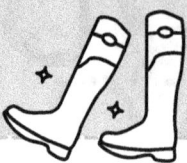

What went well:

* _____
* _____
* _____
* _____
* _____

What I need to practise:

1. _____
   _____
2. _____
   _____
3. _____

Pony of the week

THIS WEEK I HAVE ...

- ○ Groomed
- ○ Cleaned tack
- ○ Mucked out
- ○ Had a lesson
- ○ Helped with feeding
- ○ Been for a hack
- ○ Learnt something new
- ○ Ridden a different pony

MY LESSON TRACKER

Name: _____

Age: _____

- ○ Mare
- ○ Gelding

WANTED

★★★ DEAD or ALIVE ★★★

REWARD $ 100,000

Design your own cowboy boots

Cowboy boots have super fancy designs on them. Design your own pair of boots here!

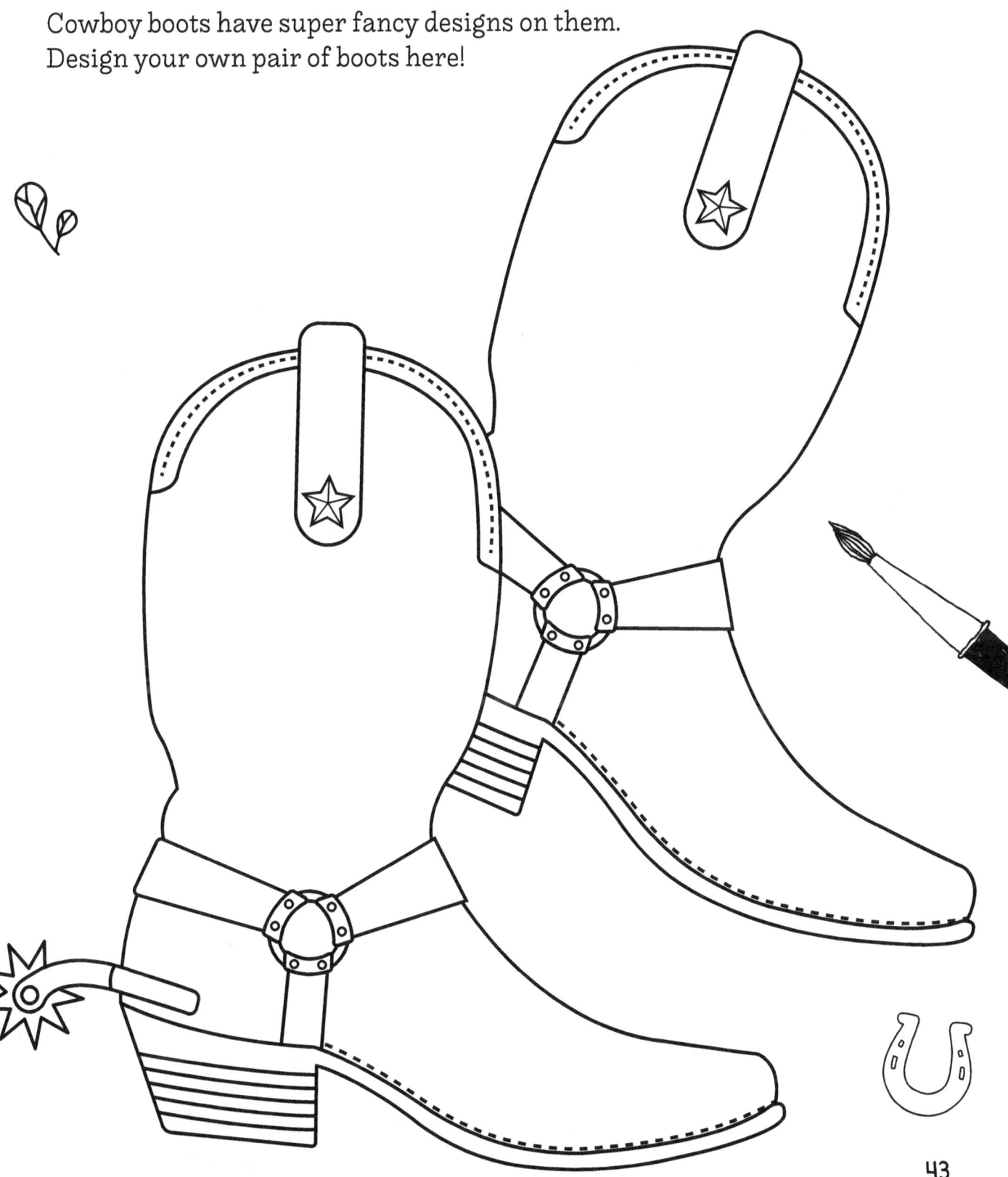

HORSE COLOURS AND HOW TO IDENTIFY THEM

Provide this handy translator to any non-horsey friends and family so they can help get the right ponies in from the field.

Bay	A brown horse.
Black	A black horse. On closer inspection, it will probably turn out to be brown.
Brown	A brown horse. What else would it be?
Chestnut	Another brown horse. Or the weird lumpy thing on the inside of the horses' leg. You'll have to work out which one we mean.
Liver chestnut	Yup, brown again.
Dun	A brown horse with a black wig.
Grey	Any colour except grey, most frequently mud coloured. Or yellow ... ewww. Also used for white horses, which makes no sense to anyone.
Palamino	A brown horse with highlights.
Piebald	Please check if it really is a horse. Equally likely to be a large dalmatian.
Skewbald	Cow impersonator.

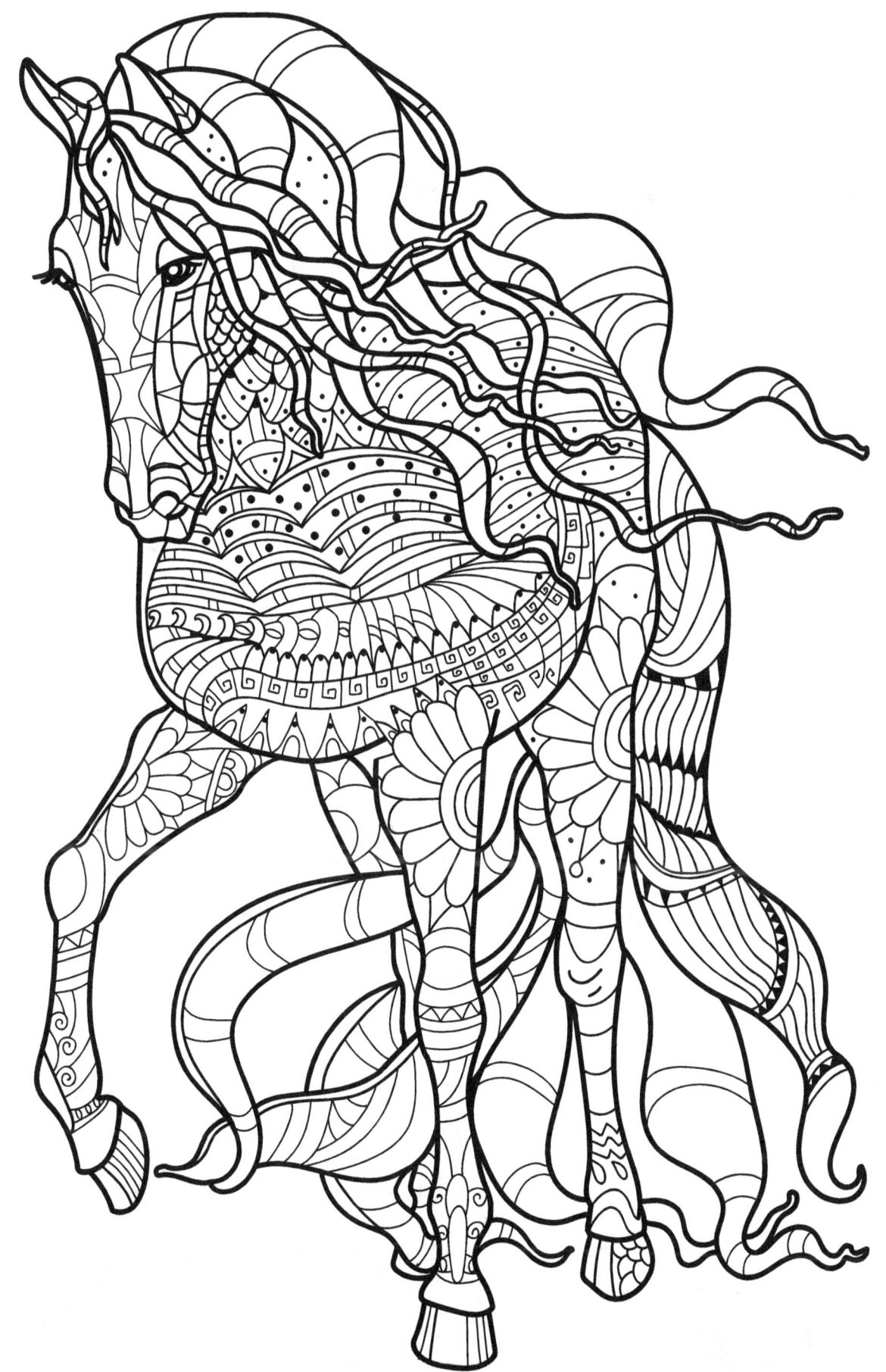

MONTH: ....

My riding goals

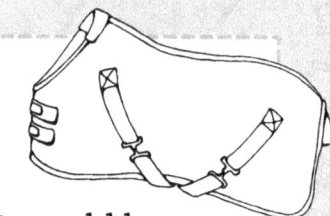

What would you like to do better or learn? For example, it could be to keep your heels down, develop a deeper seat, master the half halt, improve your jumping, ride a perfect leg yield, or maybe even try a piaffe.

Make a list of the things you want to focus on this month. If you're not sure what to pick, ask your instructor.

Goal 1: _____
_____
_____

Goal 2: _____
_____
_____

Goal 3: _____
_____
_____

I .... do hereby commit to practising these things every time I ride.

Signed: ....

Date: ....

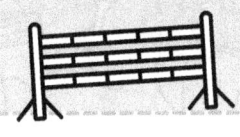

Using a goal tracker can help you achieve your targets.

GOAL	Colour in a horseshoe every time you practise
1	
2	
3	

Write or draw your goals!

WEEK ONE

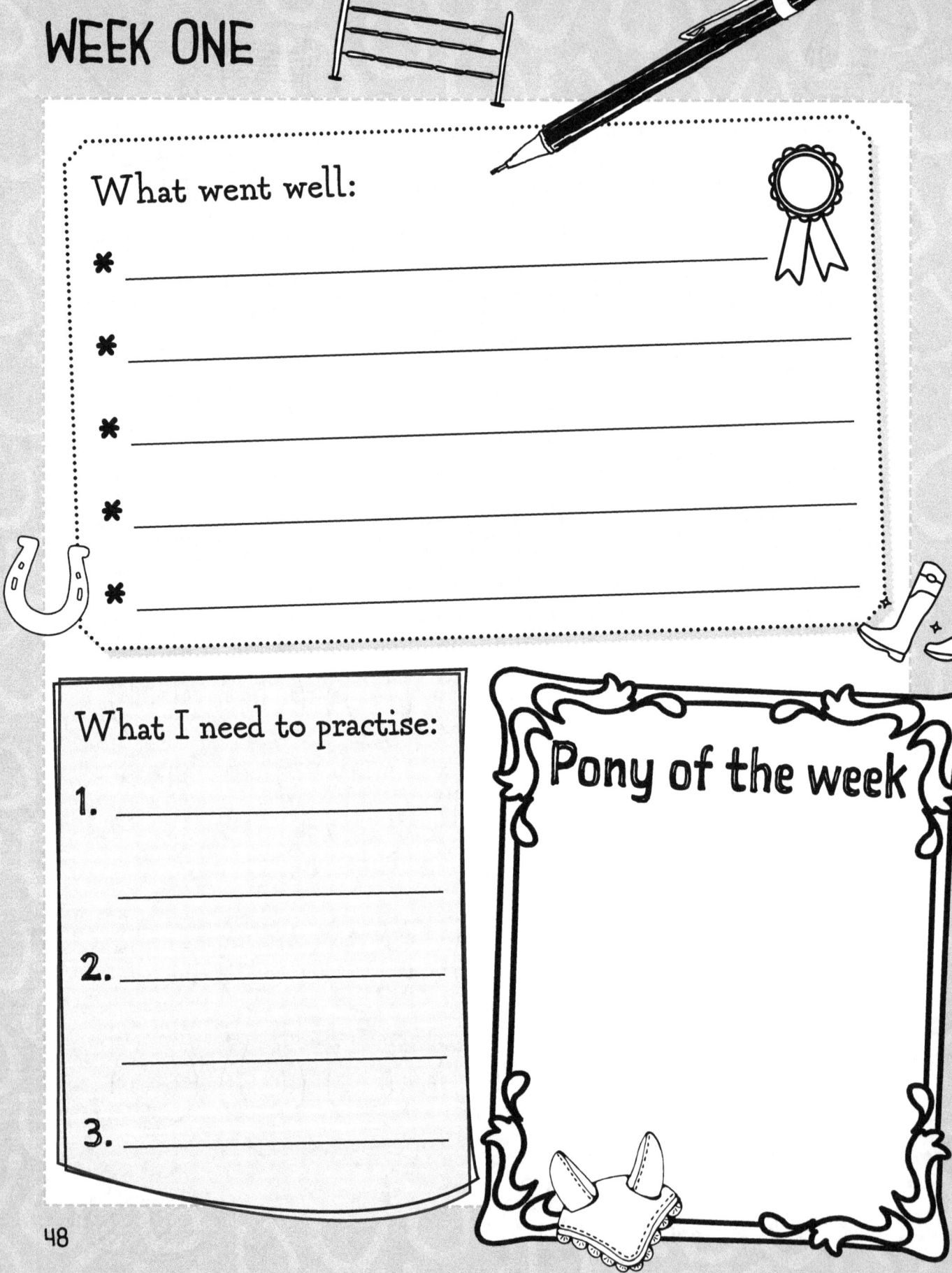

What went well:

* _____
* _____
* _____
* _____
* _____

What I need to practise:

1. _____
   _____

2. _____
   _____

3. _____

Pony of the week

THIS WEEK I HAVE ...

- ○ Groomed
- ○ Cleaned tack
- ○ Mucked out
- ○ Had a lesson
- ○ Helped with feeding
- ○ Been for a hack
- ○ Learnt something new
- ○ Ridden a different pony

MY LESSON TRACKER

Name: _____

Age: _____

○ Mare

○ Gelding

VROOOmmmm

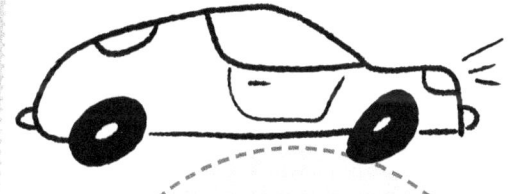

Q: What do you get if you cross a wild horse with a car?
A: A mustang convertible!

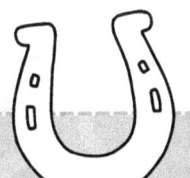

49

WEEK TWO

What went well:

* _____
* _____
* _____
* _____
* _____

What I need to practise:

1. _____
   _____
2. _____
   _____
3. _____

Pony of the week

THIS WEEK I HAVE ...

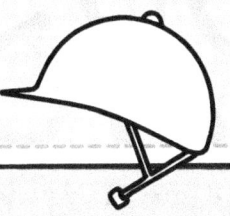

- ○ Groomed
- ○ Cleaned tack
- ○ Mucked out
- ○ Had a lesson
- ○ Helped with feeding
- ○ Been for a hack
- ○ Learnt something new
- ○ Ridden a different pony

MY LESSON TRACKER

Name: _____

Age: _____

○ Mare

○ Gelding

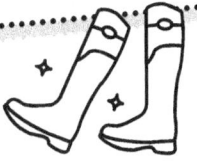
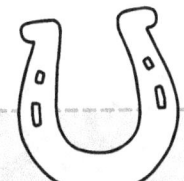
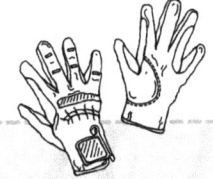

THIS WEEK I HAVE ...

- ○ Groomed
- ○ Cleaned tack
- ○ Mucked out
- ○ Had a lesson
- ○ Helped with feeding
- ○ Been for a hack
- ○ Learnt something new
- ○ Ridden a different pony

MY LESSON TRACKER

Name: _____

Age: _____

○ Mare

○ Gelding

Did you know?
The fear of horses is known as *equinophobia*.

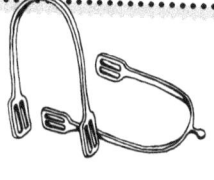

BOO!

WEEK FOUR

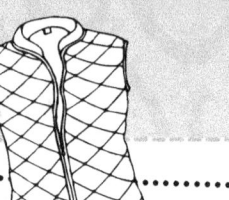
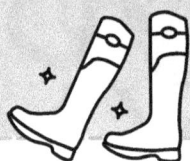

What went well:

* _____
* _____
* _____
* _____
* _____

What I need to practise:

1. _____
   _____
2. _____
   _____
3. _____

Pony of the week

THIS WEEK I HAVE ...

- ◯ Groomed
- ◯ Cleaned tack
- ◯ Mucked out
- ◯ Had a lesson
- ◯ Helped with feeding
- ◯ Been for a hack
- ◯ Learnt something new
- ◯ Ridden a different pony

MY LESSON TRACKER

Name: _____

Age: _____

- ◯ Mare
- ◯ Gelding

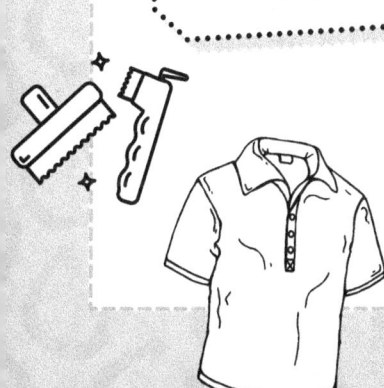

Decorative storage jars

Tidy your room with these horsey jars!

1. Stick the horse(s) to the centre of the lid with strong glue.

You will need
* A glass jar with a lid
* Spray paint in whatever colour you want the lid and horse to be
* Tiny plastic toy horses
* Strong glue

These make great gifts for any pony-mad friends!

2. Lay out some newspaper to protect the surface then carefully spray paint the lid and the plastic horse. It's better to do this outside because of the paint fumes.

3. Let it dry completely before you touch it.

CATCH PHRASE

How many of these does your trainer say in one lesson? Ask a non-riding friend to keep score.

Score 1 point for each instruction.

- Look up!
- Breathe
- Heels down
- Wrong lead
- Leg!
- Inside leg
- Don't turn too early
- Outside rein
- Shorten your reins
- Bend
- Sit up!
- Keep your hands still
- That's not a circle
- Change your diagonal
- More leg!
- Stop flapping your legs
- Turn sooner
- They're not listening to you
- Let's try that again
- Half halt!

My Score:

MONTH: ....

My riding goals

 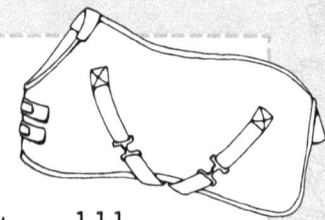

What would you like to do better or learn? For example, it could be to keep your heels down, develop a deeper seat, master the half halt, improve your jumping, ride a perfect leg yield, or maybe even try a *piaffe*.

Make a list of the things you want to focus on this month. If you're not sure what to pick, ask your instructor.

Goal 1: _____
_____
_____

Goal 2: _____
_____
_____

Goal 3: _____
_____
_____

I ....
do hereby commit to practising these things every time I ride.

Signed: ....
Date: ....

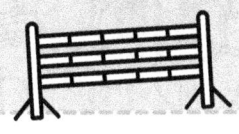

Using a goal tracker can help you achieve your targets.

GOAL	Colour in a horseshoe every time you practise
1	
2	
3	

Write or draw your goals!

WEEK ONE

What went well:

* _____
* _____
* _____
* _____
* _____

What I need to practise:

1. _____
   _____
2. _____
   _____
3. _____

Pony of the week

THIS WEEK I HAVE ...

- ○ Groomed
- ○ Cleaned tack
- ○ Mucked out
- ○ Had a lesson
- ○ Helped with feeding
- ○ Been for a hack
- ○ Learnt something new
- ○ Ridden a different pony

MY LESSON TRACKER

Name: _____

Age: _____

○ Mare

○ Gelding

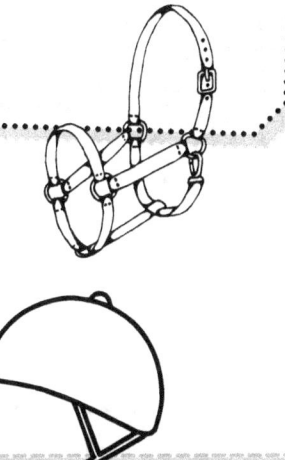

Q: What do race horses eat?
A: Fast Food!

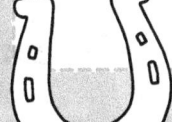

WEEK TWO

What went well:

* _____
* _____
* _____
* _____
* _____

What I need to practise:

1. _____

2. _____

3. _____

Pony of the week

THIS WEEK I HAVE ...

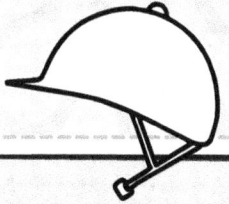

- ○ Groomed
- ○ Cleaned tack
- ○ Mucked out
- ○ Had a lesson
- ○ Helped with feeding
- ○ Been for a hack
- ○ Learnt something new
- ○ Ridden a different pony

MY LESSON TRACKER

Name: _____

Age: _____

○ Mare

○ Gelding

WEEK THREE

What went well:

* _____
* _____
* _____
* _____
* _____

What I need to practise:

1. _____
2. _____
3. _____

Pony of the week

THIS WEEK I HAVE ...

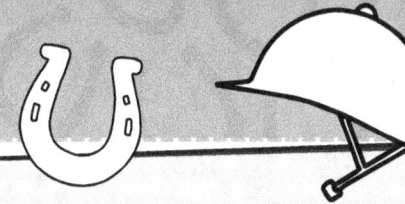

- ○ Groomed
- ○ Cleaned tack
- ○ Mucked out
- ○ Had a lesson
- ○ Helped with feeding
- ○ Been for a hack
- ○ Learnt something new
- ○ Ridden a different pony

MY LESSON TRACKER

Name: _____

Age: _____

○ Mare

○ Gelding

Did you know?

The smallest horse ever recorded was called Thumbelina. She was only 14 inches/ 45 cm tall.

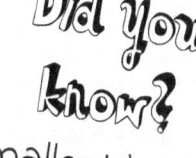
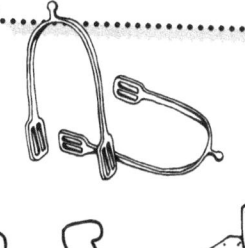
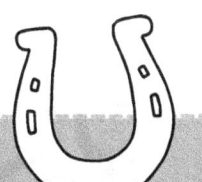

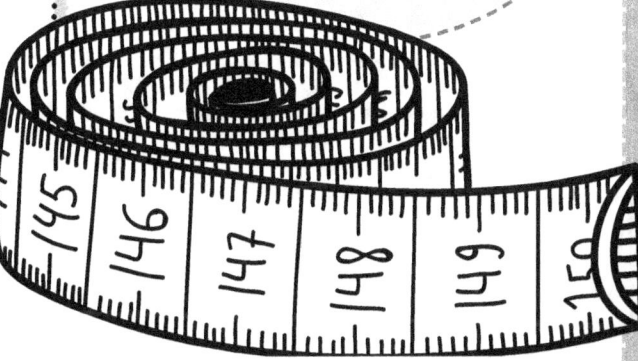

WEEK FOUR

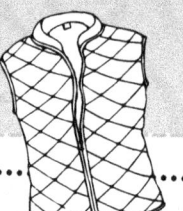

What went well:

* _____
* _____
* _____
* _____
* _____

What I need to practise:

1. _____

2. _____

3. _____

Pony of the week

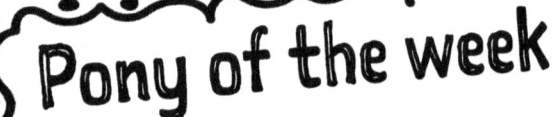

THIS WEEK I HAVE ...

- ◯ Groomed
- ◯ Cleaned tack
- ◯ Mucked out
- ◯ Had a lesson
- ◯ Helped with feeding
- ◯ Been for a hack
- ◯ Learnt something new
- ◯ Ridden a different pony

MY LESSON TRACKER

Name: _____

Age: _____

◯ Mare

◯ Gelding

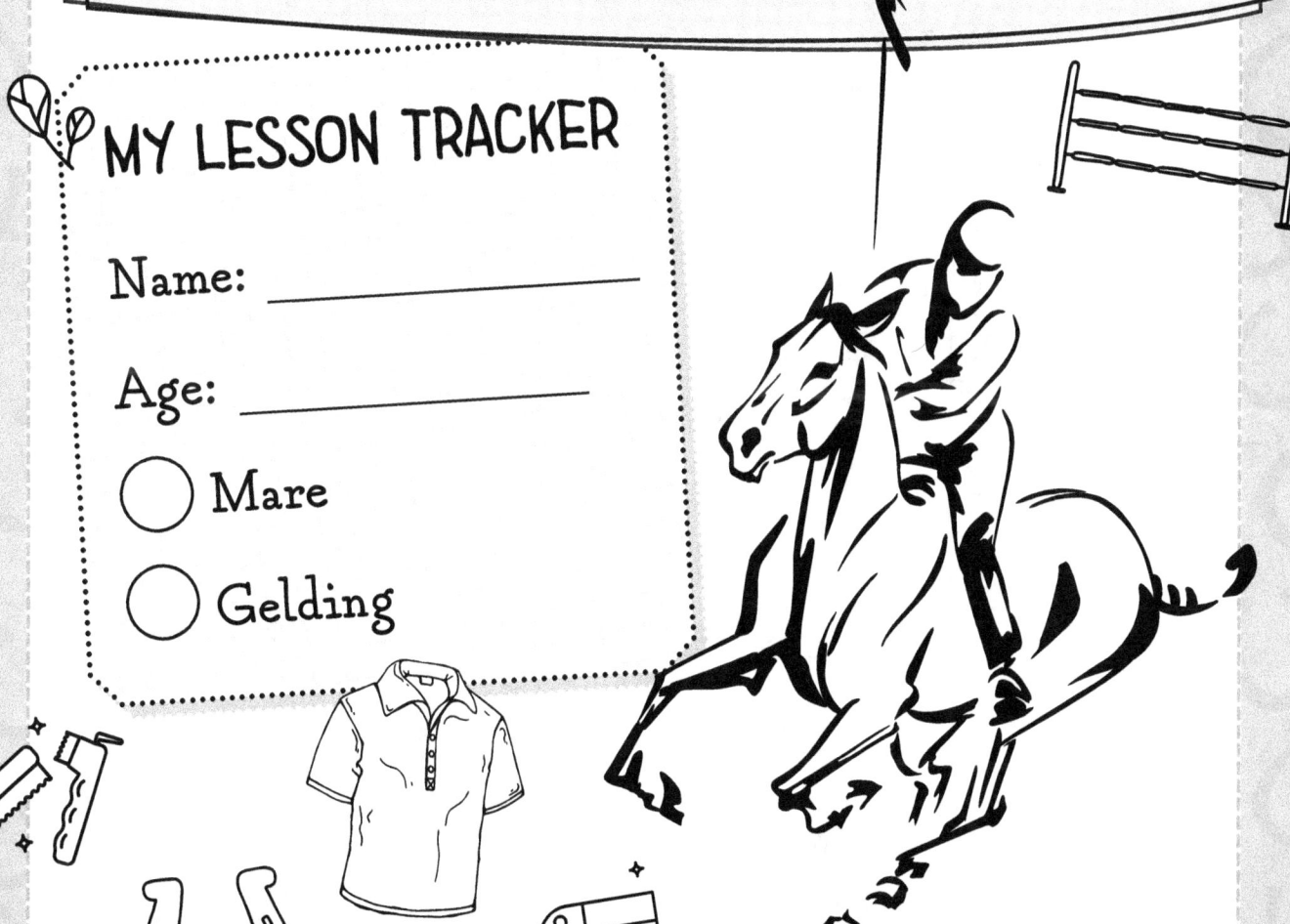

Hungry as a Horse

S	C	W	K	O	S	B	Q	L	H	K	N	E	S	A	R	T	Z
P	Y	O	H	G	T	E	W	M	S	V	V	V	L	H	A	O	V
E	Y	Q	R	B	Y	G	S	L	X	X	T	F	U	B	Z	Q	G
D	B	F	P	N	J	R	M	S	O	W	A	Y	K	V	F	F	O
S	E	L	P	P	A	A	T	R	A	L	L	S	B	Y	F	U	Y
Z	X	Z	Z	P	Y	S	V	U	F	L	U	V	N	U	I	W	T
W	H	O	U	E	C	S	J	A	D	J	O	G	R	A	F	N	B
T	B	I	O	R	F	X	U	N	B	I	C	M	R	W	I	S	K
V	H	S	Y	G	Q	U	R	O	X	A	P	C	L	E	T	C	W
U	S	F	Y	S	N	U	H	I	F	Z	X	V	C	O	J	X	K
X	Y	C	V	Z	A	M	W	H	G	Y	C	D	R	E	Z	O	D
R	I	O	L	T	X	R	Q	F	V	C	E	R	J	L	K	T	B
C	M	J	N	J	T	X	Z	Z	V	D	A	L	C	H	A	F	F
I	U	Z	X	L	U	N	I	Q	V	C	U	T	R	H	X	H	S
F	E	G	A	L	Y	A	H	J	S	B	B	M	B	A	A	W	T
S	E	S	U	G	A	R	B	E	E	T	Y	O	Q	Y	B	K	A
Y	T	B	L	U	K	B	E	X	B	O	O	X	M	C	Q	O	O
D	Z	B	B	X	F	E	R	A	F	E	H	G	G	S	T	Q	Z

- ALFALFA
- BRAN
- CORN
- HAYLAGE
- SALT
- APPLES
- CARROTS
- GRASS
- MOLASSES
- SUGARBEET
- BARLEY
- CHAFF
- HAY
- OATS

Answers on page 172

HAVE YOU EVER ...

- ☐ Fallen over in the muck heap?
- ☐ Worn jodhpurs to a party?
- ☐ Lost a boot in the mud?
- ☐ Fallen off a horse?
- ☐ Chased a horse round a field trying to catch it?
- ☐ Put a rug on back to front?
- ☐ Got lost during a dressage test?
- ☐ Completed a jump without your pony?
- ☐ Cleaned the bit on your shirt?
- ☐ Misidentified your horse from afar?
- ☐ Wondered if you can train a dog to do a flying change?
- ☐ Learnt the wrong test?
- ☐ Changed your route on a hack to avoid having to open a gate?
- ☐ Licked a salt lick?
- ☐ Shared an apple with a pony?
- ☐ Clicked at someone to get them to hurry up?
- ☐ Used horse shampoo, conditioner or shine spray on your own hair?
- ☐ Found straw in your hair several hours after you left the stables?
- ☐ Spent so long chatting at the yard that you ran out of time to ride, gave the pony a carrot, and went home?
- ☐ Hit yourself in the face whilst trying to do up a girth?
- ☐ Run more yourself when lunging than the pony did?

Score 1 point for each question you answered "yes" to.

What did you score?

0
Welcome to the world of ponies! It won't take you long to start ticking off the items on this list. Have fun!

1 to 5
By now, your friends and family probably describe you as "horse mad". Don't worry if people laugh when you fall over in the muck heap though, they're laughing with you, not at you. We've all done it!

6 to 10
It's time to put up a sign on your bedroom door saying, "I'm probably at the stables". Don't forget the number one rule: safety first.

11 or more
Yee hah! You are officially a fully qualified member of the "I ♡ ponies" club. Remember to help people who have less experience than you.

MONTH: ....

My riding goals

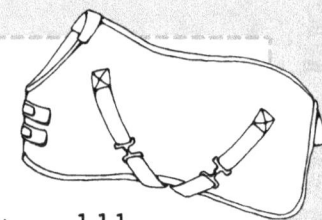

What would you like to do better or learn? For example, it could be to keep your heels down, develop a deeper seat, master the half halt, improve your jumping, ride a perfect leg yield, or maybe even try a *piaffe*.

Make a list of the things you want to focus on this month. If you're not sure what to pick, ask your instructor.

Goal 1: _____

_____

_____

Goal 2: _____

_____

_____

Goal 3: _____

_____

_____

I .... do hereby commit to practising these things every time I ride.

Signed: ....

Date: ....

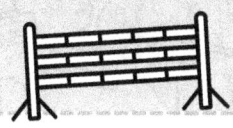

Using a goal tracker can help you achieve your targets.

GOAL	Colour in a horseshoe every time you practise
1	
2	
3	

Write or draw your goals!

WEEK ONE

What went well:

* _____
* _____
* _____
* _____
* _____

What I need to practise:

1. _____
2. _____
3. _____

Pony of the week

THIS WEEK I HAVE ...

- ○ Groomed
- ○ Cleaned tack
- ○ Mucked out
- ○ Had a lesson
- ○ Helped with feeding
- ○ Been for a hack
- ○ Learnt something new
- ○ Ridden a different pony

MY LESSON TRACKER

Name: _____

Age: _____

○ Mare

○ Gelding

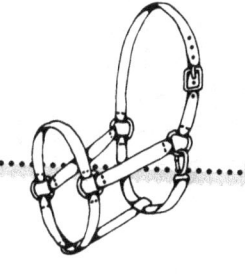

Q: What's a horse's favourite sport?
A: Stable tennis!

WEEK TWO

What went well:

* _____
* _____
* _____
* _____
* _____

What I need to practise:

1. _____

2. _____

3. _____

Pony of the week

THIS WEEK I HAVE ...

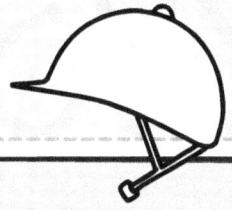

- ◯ Groomed
- ◯ Cleaned tack
- ◯ Mucked out
- ◯ Had a lesson
- ◯ Helped with feeding
- ◯ Been for a hack
- ◯ Learnt something new
- ◯ Ridden a different pony

MY LESSON TRACKER

Name: _____

Age: _____

◯ Mare

◯ Gelding

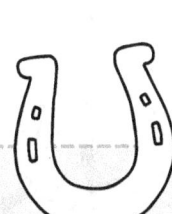

WEEK THREE

What went well:

* _____
* _____
* _____
* _____
* _____

What I need to practise:

1. _____
2. _____
3. _____

Pony of the week

THIS WEEK I HAVE ...

- ○ Groomed
- ○ Cleaned tack
- ○ Mucked out
- ○ Had a lesson
- ○ Helped with feeding
- ○ Been for a hack
- ○ Learnt something new
- ○ Ridden a different pony

MY LESSON TRACKER

Name: _____

Age: _____

○ Mare

○ Gelding

Did you know?

A horse's ears point where it is looking, so if they point in two directions, it's looking at two different things at the same time.

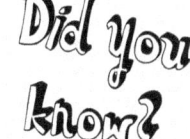
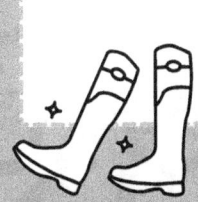

WEEK FOUR

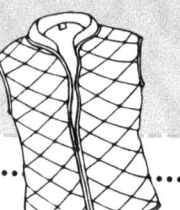

What went well:

* _____
* _____
* _____
* _____
* _____

What I need to practise:

1. _____
   _____

2. _____
   _____

3. _____

Pony of the week

THIS WEEK I HAVE ...

- ○ Groomed
- ○ Cleaned tack
- ○ Mucked out
- ○ Had a lesson
- ○ Helped with feeding
- ○ Been for a hack
- ○ Learnt something new
- ○ Ridden a different pony

MY LESSON TRACKER

Name: _____

Age: _____

- ○ Mare
- ○ Gelding

Horse clothes and how to wear them

Provide this handy translator to any non-horsey friends and family so they can get the ponies dressed appropriately for the planned activity.

Bandages = Socks

Rubber ring = Ankle bracelet

Over-reach boots = Hiking shoes

Brushing boots = Shin pads

Fly veil = Hat

Browband = Tiara

Numnah = Cushion

Girth = Belt

Reins = Ineffective steering wheel

GP = General purpose saddle. Usually accompanied by a dressage saddle and a jump saddle, calling into question the accuracy of the name

LABEL THE POINTS OF A HORSE

- Muzzle
- Jugular gland
- Forearm
- Knee
- Coronet
- Hoof
- Fetlock
- Shoulder
- Point of buttock
- Pastern
- Hock
- Dock
- Croup
- Stifle
- Withers
- Crest
- Poll
- Point of hip

Answers on page 172

MONTH: ....

My riding goals

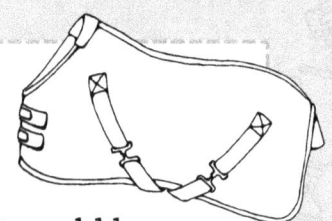

What would you like to do better or learn? For example, it could be to keep your heels down, develop a deeper seat, master the half halt, improve your jumping, ride a perfect leg yield, or maybe even try a *piaffe*.

Make a list of the things you want to focus on this month. If you're not sure what to pick, ask your instructor.

Goal 1: _____

_____

_____

Goal 2: _____

_____

_____

Goal 3: _____

_____

_____

I .... do hereby commit to practising these things every time I ride.

Signed: ....

Date: ....

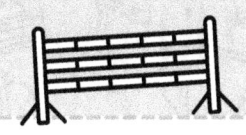

Using a goal tracker can help you achieve your targets.

GOAL	Colour in a horseshoe every time you practise
1	
2	
3	

Write or draw your goals!

WEEK ONE

What went well:

* _____
* _____
* _____
* _____
* _____

What I need to practise:

1. _____
   _____

2. _____
   _____

3. _____

Pony of the week

THIS WEEK I HAVE ...

- ◯ Groomed
- ◯ Cleaned tack
- ◯ Mucked out
- ◯ Had a lesson
- ◯ Helped with feeding
- ◯ Been for a hack
- ◯ Learnt something new
- ◯ Ridden a different pony

MY LESSON TRACKER

Name: _____

Age: _____

- ◯ Mare
- ◯ Gelding

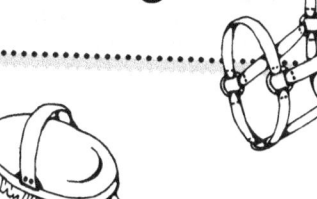
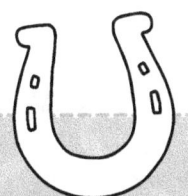
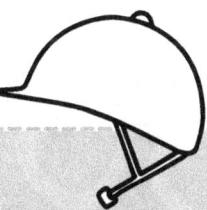

Q: What is a horse's favourite hair style?
A: Pony tail!

WEEK TWO

What went well:

* _____
* _____
* _____
* _____
* _____

What I need to practise:

1. _____
2. _____
3. _____

Pony of the week

THIS WEEK I HAVE ...

- ◯ Groomed
- ◯ Cleaned tack
- ◯ Mucked out
- ◯ Had a lesson
- ◯ Helped with feeding
- ◯ Been for a hack
- ◯ Learnt something new
- ◯ Ridden a different pony

MY LESSON TRACKER

Name:

Age: _____

- ◯ Mare
- ◯ Gelding

WEEK THREE

What went well:

* _____
* _____
* _____
* _____
* _____

What I need to practise:

1. _____
2. _____
3. _____

Pony of the week

THIS WEEK I HAVE ...

- ○ Groomed
- ○ Cleaned tack
- ○ Mucked out
- ○ Had a lesson
- ○ Helped with feeding
- ○ Been for a hack
- ○ Learnt something new
- ○ Ridden a different pony

MY LESSON TRACKER

Name: _____

Age: _____

○ Mare

○ Gelding

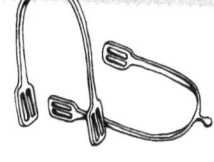

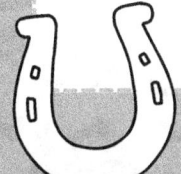

Did you know?
The national animal of Scotland is the unicorn.

WEEK FOUR

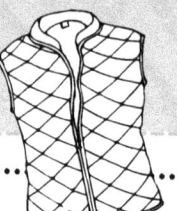

What went well:

* _____
* _____
* _____
* _____
* _____

What I need to practise:

1. _____
   _____
2. _____
   _____
3. _____

Pony of the week

THIS WEEK I HAVE ...

- ◯ Groomed
- ◯ Cleaned tack
- ◯ Mucked out
- ◯ Had a lesson
- ◯ Helped with feeding
- ◯ Been for a hack
- ◯ Learnt something new
- ◯ Ridden a different pony

MY LESSON TRACKER

Name: _____

Age: _____

- ◯ Mare
- ◯ Gelding

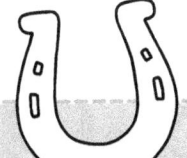

TRAINER TRANSLATOR

Provide this handy translator to any non-horsey friends and family before they watch your riding lesson.

"More leg" — Often followed by "Leg, leg, leg." This is the answer to almost every scenario, including those when common sense would suggest adding leg must surely be ill-advised.

"He/she's a bit fresh" — Pony is being an idiot.

"Half halt" — Brake.

"Another half halt" — Brake harder.

"It's quite a big course, you're going to need to hunt round" — There's pretty much no hope. Just sit up, give it a kick, and hope for the best.

"Stop fiddling with the reins" — You're clinging on for dear life.

"Try and get a deeper stride next time" — You were on such a flyer you need a passport and boarding card.

"Steady" — This isn't point-to-point, slow down!

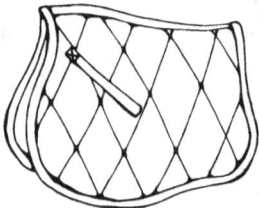

AMAZING MAZE

Can you help the pony to the carrot?

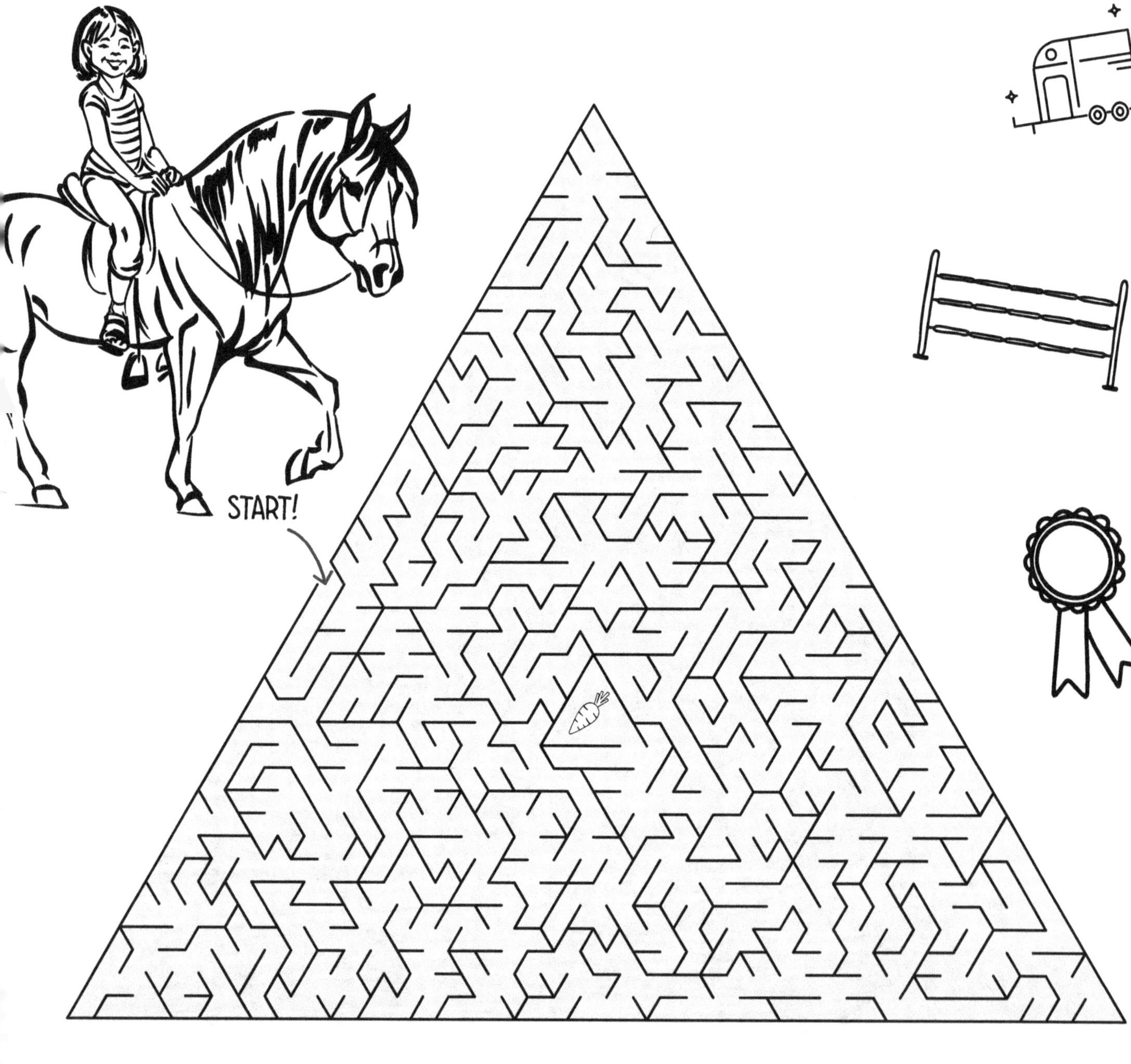

START!

Answers on page 172

MONTH: ....

My riding goals

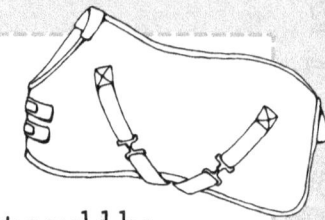

What would you like to do better or learn? For example, it could be to keep your heels down, develop a deeper seat, master the half halt, improve your jumping, ride a perfect leg yield, or maybe even try a *piaffe*.

Make a list of the things you want to focus on this month. If you're not sure what to pick, ask your instructor.

Goal 1: _____

_____

_____

Goal 2: _____

_____

_____

Goal 3: _____

_____

_____

I .... do hereby commit to practising these things every time I ride.

Signed: ....

Date: ....

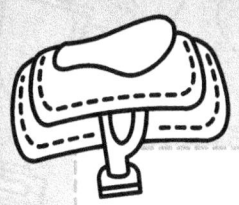
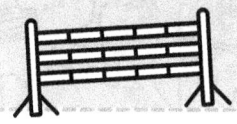

Using a goal tracker can help you achieve your targets.

GOAL	Colour in a horseshoe every time you practise
1	
2	
3	

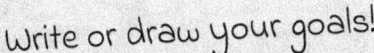

Write or draw your goals!

WEEK ONE

What went well:

* _____
* _____
* _____
* _____
* _____

What I need to practise:

1. _____

2. _____

3. _____

Pony of the week

THIS WEEK I HAVE ...

- ○ Groomed
- ○ Cleaned tack
- ○ Mucked out
- ○ Had a lesson
- ○ Helped with feeding
- ○ Been for a hack
- ○ Learnt something new
- ○ Ridden a different pony

MY LESSON TRACKER

Name: _____

Age: _____

○ Mare

○ Gelding

Q: What kind of bread does a horse eat?
A: Thoroughbred!

WEEK TWO

What went well:

* _____
* _____
* _____
* _____
* _____

What I need to practise:

1. _____
   _____
2. _____
   _____
3. _____

Pony of the week

THIS WEEK I HAVE ...

- ○ Groomed
- ○ Cleaned tack
- ○ Mucked out
- ○ Had a lesson
- ○ Helped with feeding
- ○ Been for a hack
- ○ Learnt something new
- ○ Ridden a different pony

MY LESSON TRACKER

Name: _____

Age: _____

○ Mare

○ Gelding

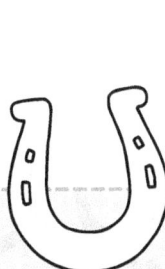

THIS WEEK I HAVE ...

- ○ Groomed
- ○ Cleaned tack
- ○ Mucked out
- ○ Had a lesson
- ○ Helped with feeding
- ○ Been for a hack
- ○ Learnt something new
- ○ Ridden a different pony

MY LESSON TRACKER

Name: _____

Age: _____

○ Mare

○ Gelding

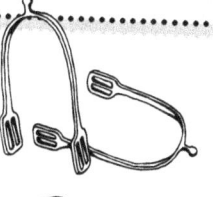
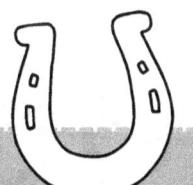

According to legend

The shoe of a two-year-old filly placed in your butter churn will stop witches stealing your butter.

WEEK FOUR

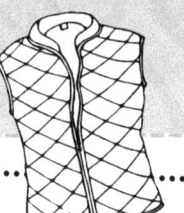
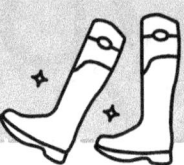

What went well:

* _____
* _____
* _____
* _____
* _____

What I need to practise:

1. _____
2. _____
3. _____

Pony of the week

THIS WEEK I HAVE ...

- ○ Groomed
- ○ Cleaned tack
- ○ Mucked out
- ○ Had a lesson
- ○ Helped with feeding
- ○ Been for a hack
- ○ Learnt something new
- ○ Ridden a different pony

MY LESSON TRACKER

Name: _____

Age: _____

- ○ Mare
- ○ Gelding

ARENA NAVIGATION

Provide this map to any non-horsey friends and family so they can help you prepare for a dressage test.

AKEHCMBF

Equestrian alphabet.
People may suggest you remember it with a handy (?) mnemonic like *All King Edward's Horses Can Manage Big Fences*. You'll still get confused though.

DLXIG

Invisible navigation points. Because that makes it so much clearer.

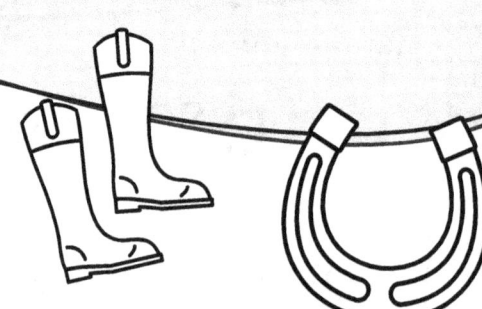

AKVESHCMRBPF

Advanced level equestrian navigation.
Or you could just shout random letters, it's unlikely anyone will notice.

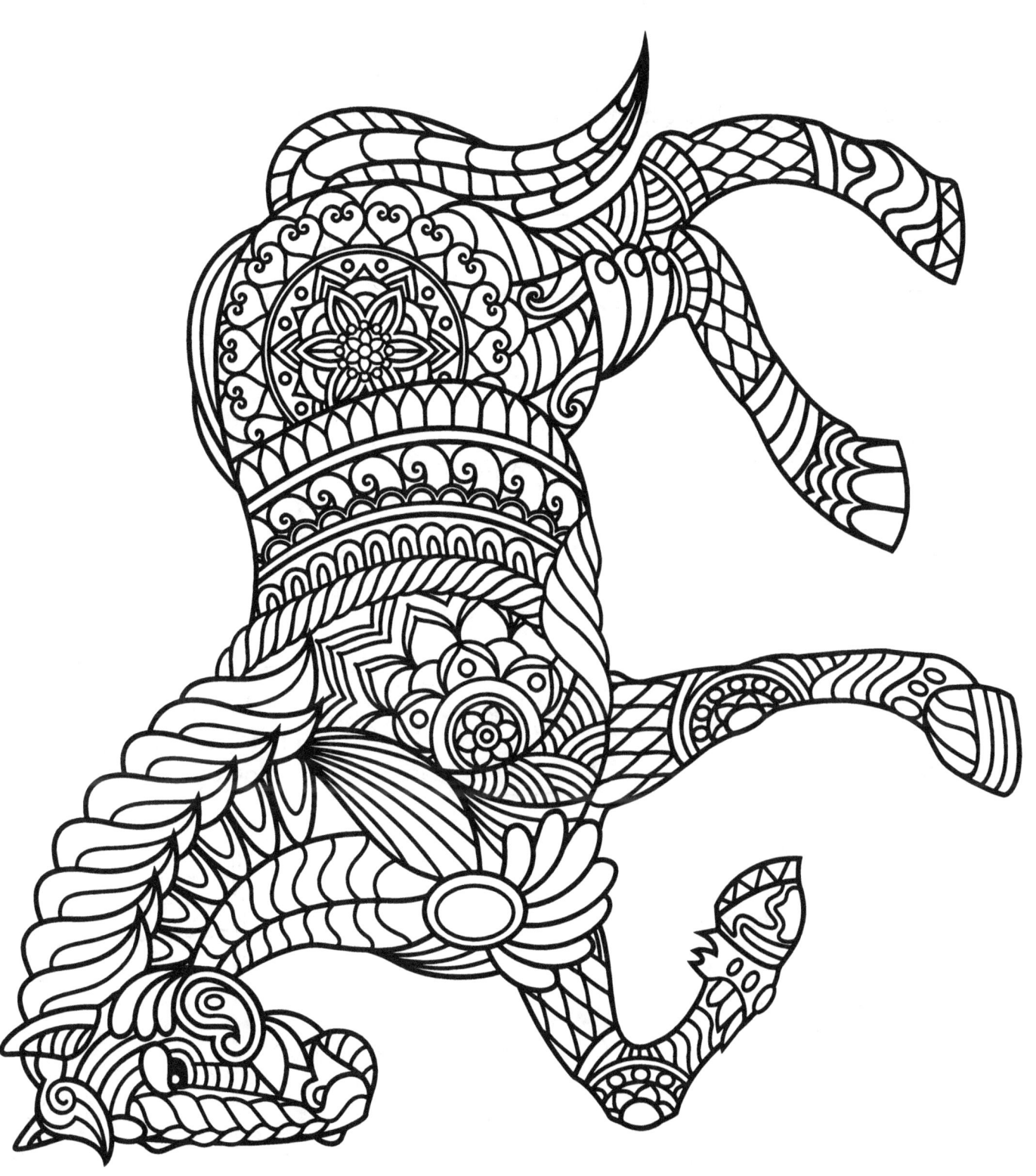

THE SIT UP MATRIX

"*Sit up...*" can be used in a variety of situations, and interpretation depends on the precise timing of the utterance as follows ...

"Sit up..." **Before you get to a fence.** This horse has a reputation for stopping.

"Sit up..." **On landing.** This horse is going to try and buck you off now.

"Sit up..." **As you go over the fence.** This horse is going to slam on the brakes when you land.

MONTH: ....

 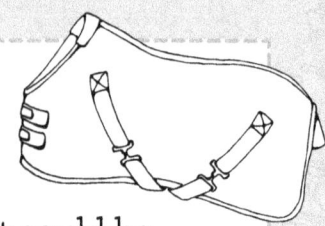

My riding goals

What would you like to do better or learn? For example, it could be to keep your heels down, develop a deeper seat, master the half halt, improve your jumping, ride a perfect leg yield, or maybe even try a *piaffe*.

Make a list of the things you want to focus on this month. If you're not sure what to pick, ask your instructor.

Goal 1: ....
....
....

Goal 2: ....
....
....

Goal 3: ....
....
....

I .... do hereby commit to practising these things every time I ride.

Signed: ....

Date: ....

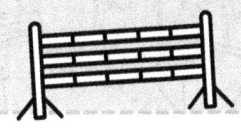

Using a goal tracker can help you achieve your targets.

GOAL	Colour in a horseshoe every time you practise
1	
2	
3	

Write or draw your goals!

WEEK ONE

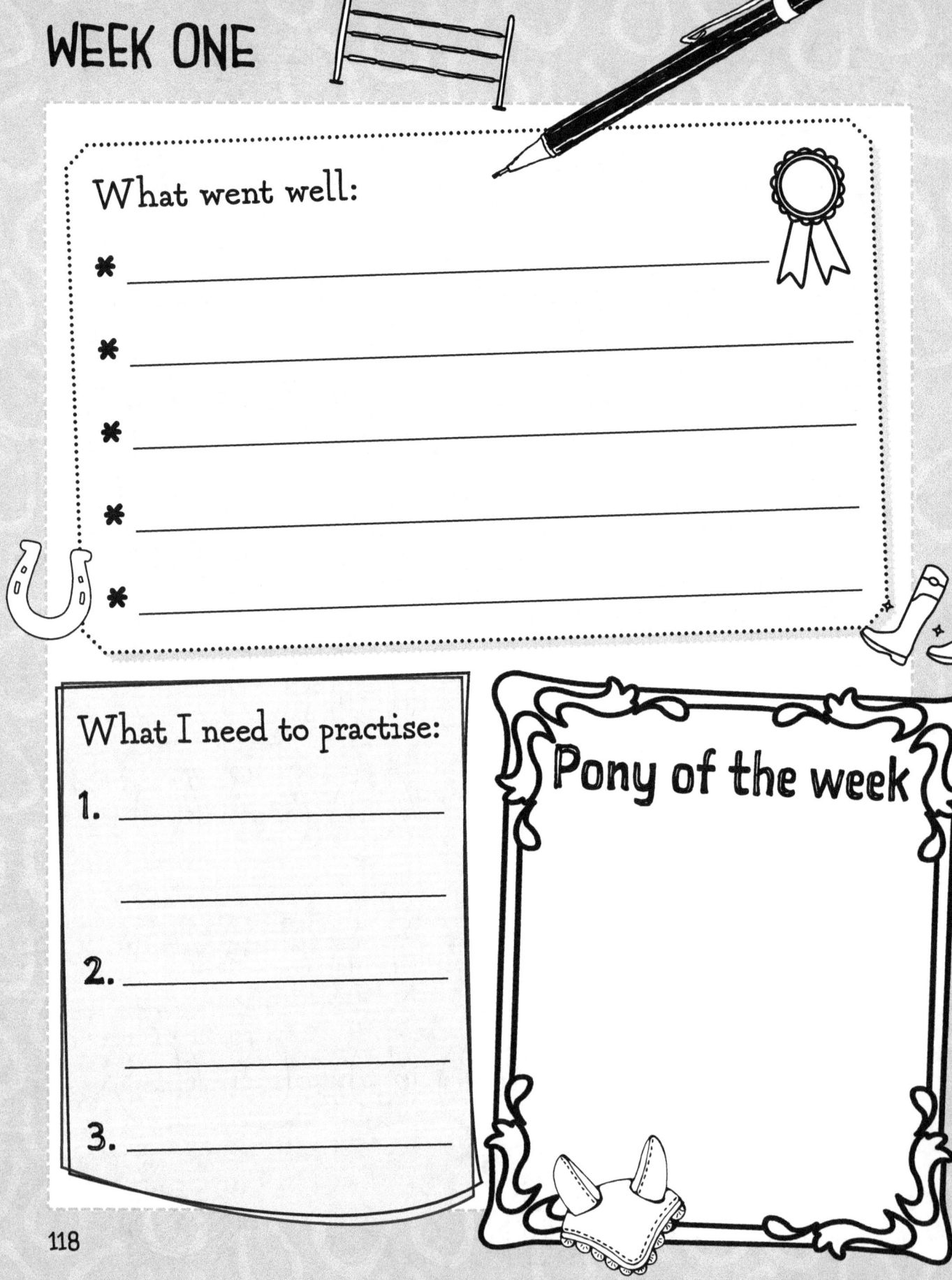

What went well:

* _____
* _____
* _____
* _____
* _____

What I need to practise:

1. _____
2. _____
3. _____

Pony of the week

THIS WEEK I HAVE ...

- ○ Groomed
- ○ Cleaned tack
- ○ Mucked out
- ○ Had a lesson
- ○ Helped with feeding
- ○ Been for a hack
- ○ Learnt something new
- ○ Ridden a different pony

MY LESSON TRACKER

Name: _____

Age: _____

○ Mare

○ Gelding

Q: Why is a tack room like a wedding?
A: There's a bridle and a groom!

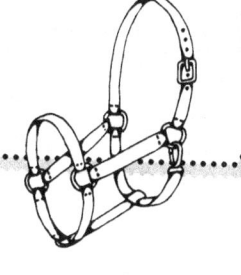

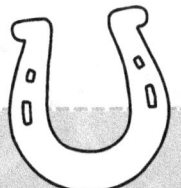

119

WEEK TWO

What went well:

* _____
* _____
* _____
* _____
* _____

What I need to practise:

1. _____
2. _____
3. _____

Pony of the week

THIS WEEK I HAVE...

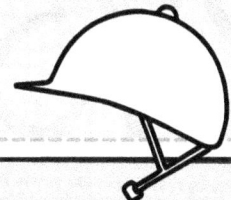

- ◯ Groomed
- ◯ Cleaned tack
- ◯ Mucked out
- ◯ Had a lesson
- ◯ Helped with feeding
- ◯ Been for a hack
- ◯ Learnt something new
- ◯ Ridden a different pony

MY LESSON TRACKER

Name: _____

Age: _____

- ◯ Mare
- ◯ Gelding

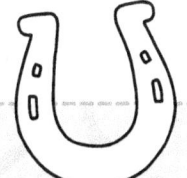
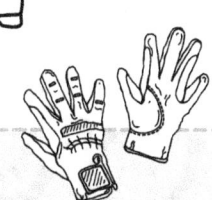

WEEK THREE

What went well:

* _____
* _____
* _____
* _____
* _____

What I need to practise:

1. _____
2. _____
3. _____

Pony of the week

THIS WEEK I HAVE ...

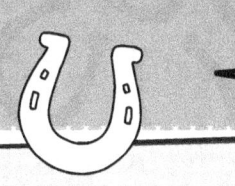

- ○ Groomed
- ○ Cleaned tack
- ○ Mucked out
- ○ Had a lesson
- ○ Helped with feeding
- ○ Been for a hack
- ○ Learnt something new
- ○ Ridden a different pony

MY LESSON TRACKER

Name: _____

Age: _____

○ Mare

○ Gelding

Did you know?

The largest horse ever recorded was a Shire horse called Sampson. He was over **21** hands/**7** feet tall at the withers.

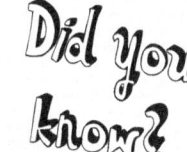
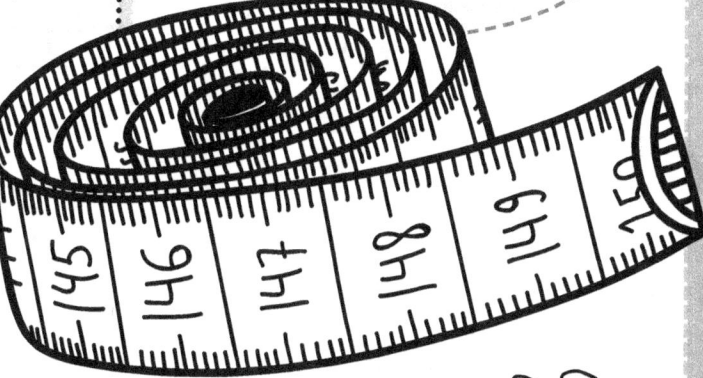
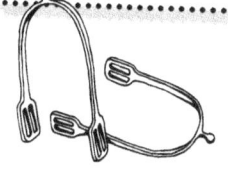

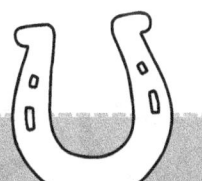

WEEK FOUR

What went well:

* _____
* _____
* _____
* _____
* _____

What I need to practise:

1. _____

   _____

2. _____

   _____

3. _____

Pony of the week

THIS WEEK I HAVE ...

- ◯ Groomed
- ◯ Cleaned tack
- ◯ Mucked out
- ◯ Had a lesson
- ◯ Helped with feeding
- ◯ Been for a hack
- ◯ Learnt something new
- ◯ Ridden a different pony

MY LESSON TRACKER

Name: _____

Age: _____

- ◯ Mare
- ◯ Gelding

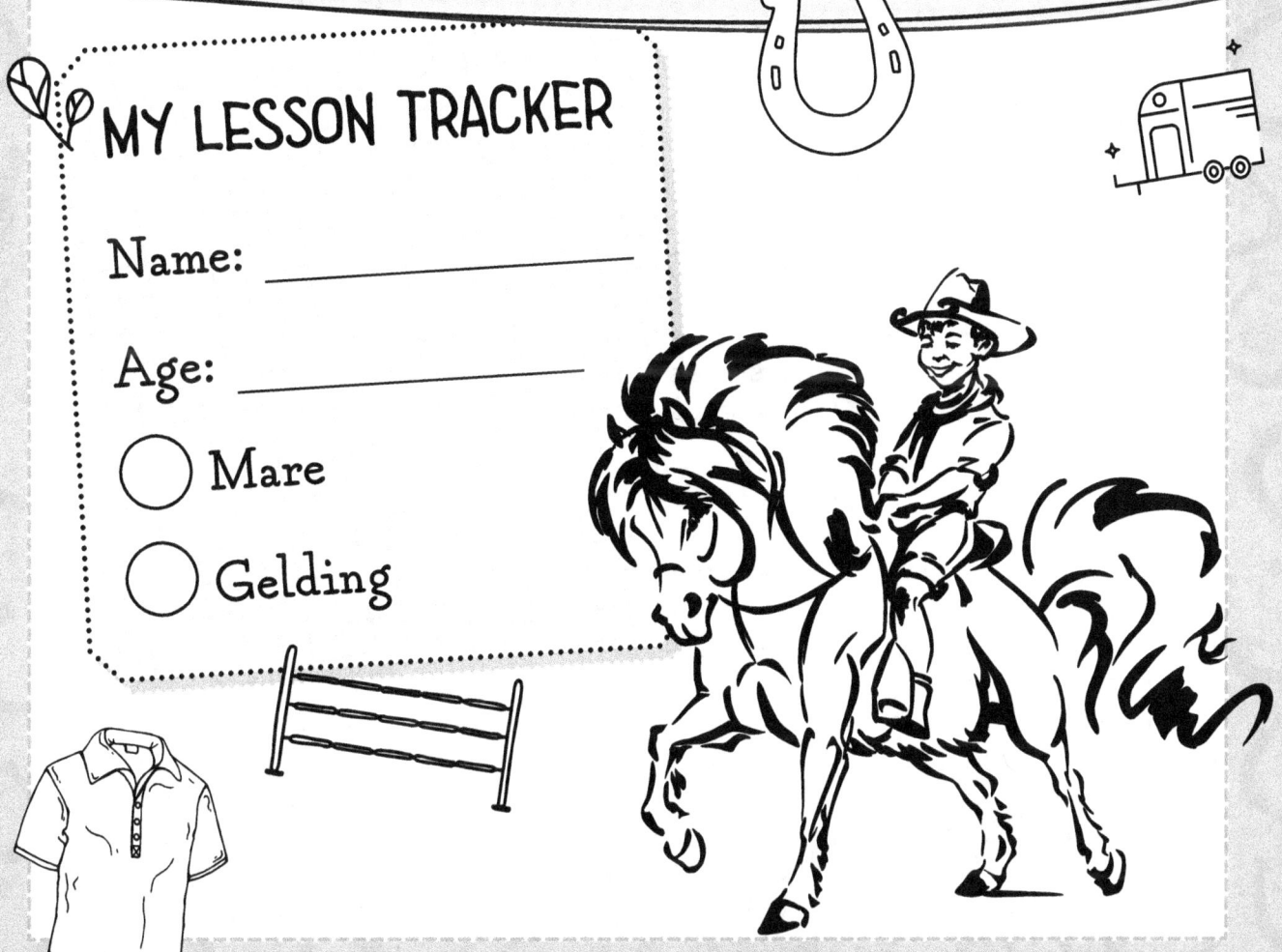

QUIZ

Circle the answer that applies to you

Would you rather
- A muck out
- B fill haynets
- C clean tack

Would you rather have
- A new brushing boots
- B new hi-viz jacket
- C new riding boots

Is the last photo you took of
- A a horse
- B a person
- C a course or test

It's raining. Do you
- A head to the stable, there's always so much to do anyway.
- B dig out a waterproof ride-on, it's only a light drizzle.
- C set up jumps or a dressage arena in your kitchen and practise a test

It's almost school holidays. Are you
- A planning long days at the yard
- B researching new bridle paths and routes
- C going to pony camp

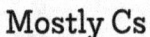

Mostly As
The Technical Guru
You're the one everyone asks for advice. From tack to grooming to feeding, your knowledge of horse care is legendary. You still like to watch the vet and the farrier when they visit so you can learn even more. When riding you're always very aware of how the horse feels and will notice the first hint of lameness or injury.

Mostly Bs
The Happy Hacker
You're the most chilled rider at the yard. Although you enjoy lessons, you're always happy to go for a hack and enjoy chatting to your friends at walk as much as the fast canters. You can navigate any obstacle with ease and map-read at a canter. When you're out, you always look after more nervous riders.

Mostly Cs
The Competition Expert
You can perfectly plait a mane at lightning speed and memorise a test quicker than you can eat a bowl of cereal. Your dedication to the sport is evidenced by a growing collection of rosettes but you're always happy to support people who have never been to a show and to clean the horse box at the end of a day out.

WHICH DOOR DO YOU OPEN?

○ Free riding lessons forever

○ A luxury horsebox

○ A stable in your garden

○ A million dollars to spend on tack and riding clothes

○ An indoor riding arena

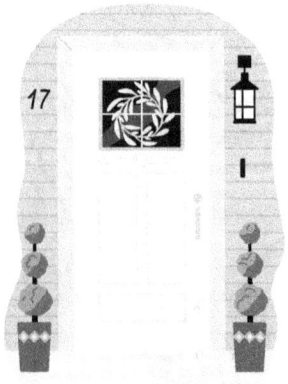
○ No vet or farrier bills ever

○ Self-cleaning stables

○ Ride every day

MONTH: ....

My riding goals

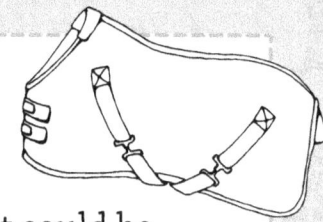

What would you like to do better or learn? For example, it could be to keep your heels down, develop a deeper seat, master the half halt, improve your jumping, ride a perfect leg yield, or maybe even try a *piaffe*.

Make a list of the things you want to focus on this month. If you're not sure what to pick, ask your instructor.

Goal 1: _____
_____
_____

Goal 2: _____
_____
_____

Goal 3: _____
_____
_____

I .... do hereby commit to practising these things every time I ride.

Signed: ....
Date: ....

130

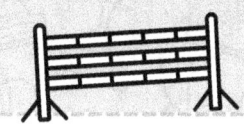

Using a goal tracker can help you achieve your targets.

GOAL	Colour in a horseshoe every time you practise
1	
2	
3	

Write or draw your goals!

WEEK ONE

What went well:

* _____
* _____
* _____
* _____
* _____

What I need to practise:

1. _____
2. _____
3. _____

Pony of the week

THIS WEEK I HAVE ...

- ◯ Groomed
- ◯ Cleaned tack
- ◯ Mucked out
- ◯ Had a lesson
- ◯ Helped with feeding
- ◯ Been for a hack
- ◯ Learnt something new
- ◯ Ridden a different pony

MY LESSON TRACKER

Name: _____

Age: _____

◯ Mare

◯ Gelding

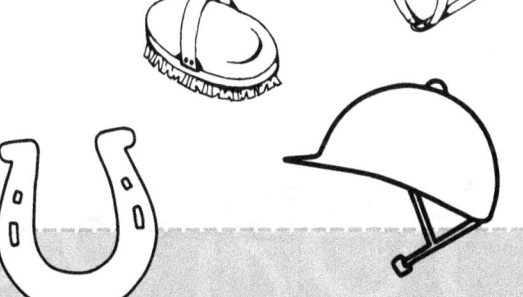

Q: When do vampires like watching horse racing?
A: When it's neck and neck.

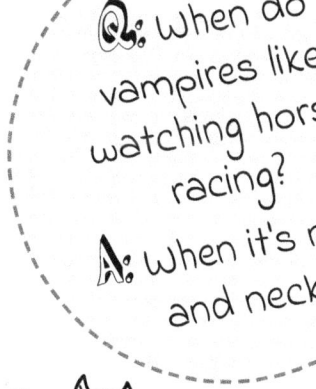

WEEK TWO

What went well:
* _____
* _____
* _____
* _____
* _____

What I need to practise:
1. _____
2. _____
3. _____

Pony of the week

THIS WEEK I HAVE ...

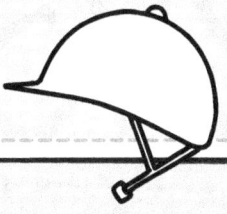

- ○ Groomed
- ○ Cleaned tack
- ○ Mucked out
- ○ Had a lesson
- ○ Helped with feeding
- ○ Been for a hack
- ○ Learnt something new
- ○ Ridden a different pony

MY LESSON TRACKER

Name: _____

Age: _____

○ Mare

○ Gelding

WEEK THREE

What went well:

* _____
* _____
* _____
* _____
* _____

What I need to practise:

1. _____
2. _____
3. _____

Pony of the week

THIS WEEK I HAVE ...

- ○ Groomed
- ○ Cleaned tack
- ○ Mucked out
- ○ Had a lesson
- ○ Helped with feeding
- ○ Been for a hack
- ○ Learnt something new
- ○ Ridden a different pony

MY LESSON TRACKER

Name: _____

Age: _____

○ Mare

○ Gelding

Did you know?
It's illegal to fish from horseback in Washington D.C.

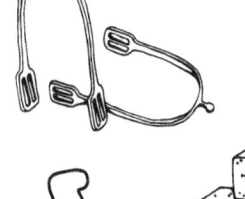

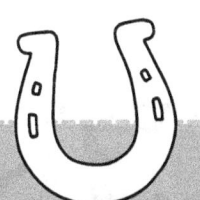

WEEK FOUR

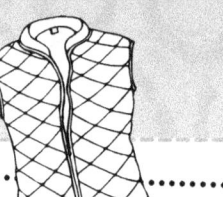
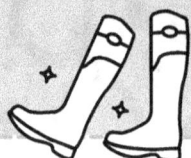

What went well:

* _____
* _____
* _____
* _____
* _____

What I need to practise:

1. _____
   _____

2. _____
   _____

3. _____

Pony of the week

THIS WEEK I HAVE ...

- ○ Groomed
- ○ Cleaned tack
- ○ Mucked out
- ○ Had a lesson
- ○ Helped with feeding
- ○ Been for a hack
- ○ Learnt something new
- ○ Ridden a different pony

MY LESSON TRACKER

Name: _____

Age: _____

○ Mare

○ Gelding

Stamping Around

Make your own horse stamps to decorate your stationery. You could even use them to make your own greeting cards or wrapping paper.

You will need
* A wooden square
* Pre-cut foam sticker ponies (any colour - it doesn't matter, but they must be identical size/shape)
* Acrylic paint/ink stamping pad

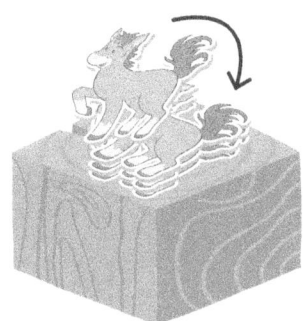

1. Remove the sticker back and apply the sticker to the middle of the wooden block.

2. Repeat, stacking two more ponies on top of the first. Depending on how thick the foam is, you will need at least three stickers so you don't get ink on the wood when you press it in the paint/ink.

Stamp away!

If you use fabric paint, you could try stamping on a plain white t-shirt.

Potions Class

Which magic potion would you drink?

MONTH: ....

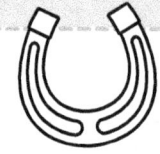
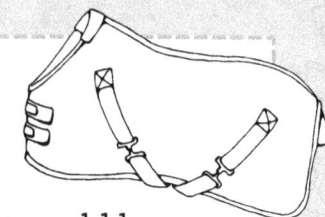

My riding goals

What would you like to do better or learn? For example, it could be to keep your heels down, develop a deeper seat, master the half halt, improve your jumping, ride a perfect leg yield, or maybe even try a *piaffe*.

Make a list of the things you want to focus on this month. If you're not sure what to pick, ask your instructor.

Goal 1: _____
_____
_____

Goal 2: _____
_____
_____

Goal 3: _____
_____
_____

I ....
do hereby commit to practising these things every time I ride.

Signed: ....
Date: ....

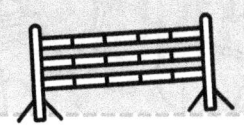

Using a goal tracker can help you achieve your targets.

GOAL	Colour in a horseshoe every time you practise
1	
2	
3	

Write or draw your goals!

WEEK ONE

What went well:

* _____
* _____
* _____
* _____
* _____

What I need to practise:

1. _____
2. _____
3. _____

Pony of the week

THIS WEEK I HAVE ...

- ○ Groomed
- ○ Cleaned tack
- ○ Mucked out
- ○ Had a lesson
- ○ Helped with feeding
- ○ Been for a hack
- ○ Learnt something new
- ○ Ridden a different pony

MY LESSON TRACKER

Name: _____

Age: _____

○ Mare

○ Gelding

Q: Why did the horse eat with its mouth open?
A: Because it had bad stable manners!

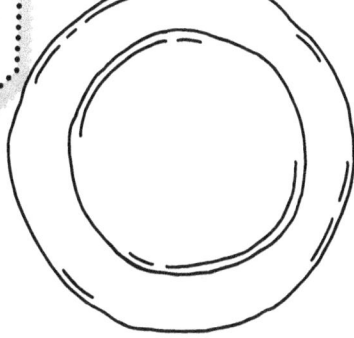

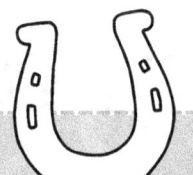

147

WEEK TWO

What went well:

* _____
* _____
* _____
* _____
* _____

What I need to practise:

1. _____

2. _____

3. _____

Pony of the week

THIS WEEK I HAVE ...

- ○ Groomed
- ○ Cleaned tack
- ○ Mucked out
- ○ Had a lesson
- ○ Helped with feeding
- ○ Been for a hack
- ○ Learnt something new
- ○ Ridden a different pony

MY LESSON TRACKER

Name: _____

Age: _____

○ Mare

○ Gelding

WEEK THREE

What went well:

* _____
* _____
* _____
* _____
* _____

What I need to practise:

1. _____
2. _____
3. _____

Pony of the week

THIS WEEK I HAVE ...

- ○ Groomed
- ○ Cleaned tack
- ○ Mucked out
- ○ Had a lesson
- ○ Helped with feeding
- ○ Been for a hack
- ○ Learnt something new
- ○ Ridden a different pony

MY LESSON TRACKER

Name: _____

Age: _____

○ Mare

○ Gelding

Did you know?

Horses have **16** muscles in each ear which allows them to rotate their ears by **180** degrees. Humans only have **3** muscles in their ears.

WEEK FOUR

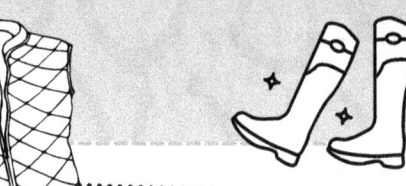

What went well:

* _____
* _____
* _____
* _____
* _____

What I need to practise:

1. _____

   _____

2. _____

   _____

3. _____

Pony of the week

THIS WEEK I HAVE ...

- ○ Groomed
- ○ Cleaned tack
- ○ Mucked out
- ○ Had a lesson
- ○ Helped with feeding
- ○ Been for a hack
- ○ Learnt something new
- ○ Ridden a different pony

MY LESSON TRACKER

Name: _____

Age: _____

○ Mare

○ Gelding

CHANGE OF REIN

Can you draw a different change of rein in each arena?

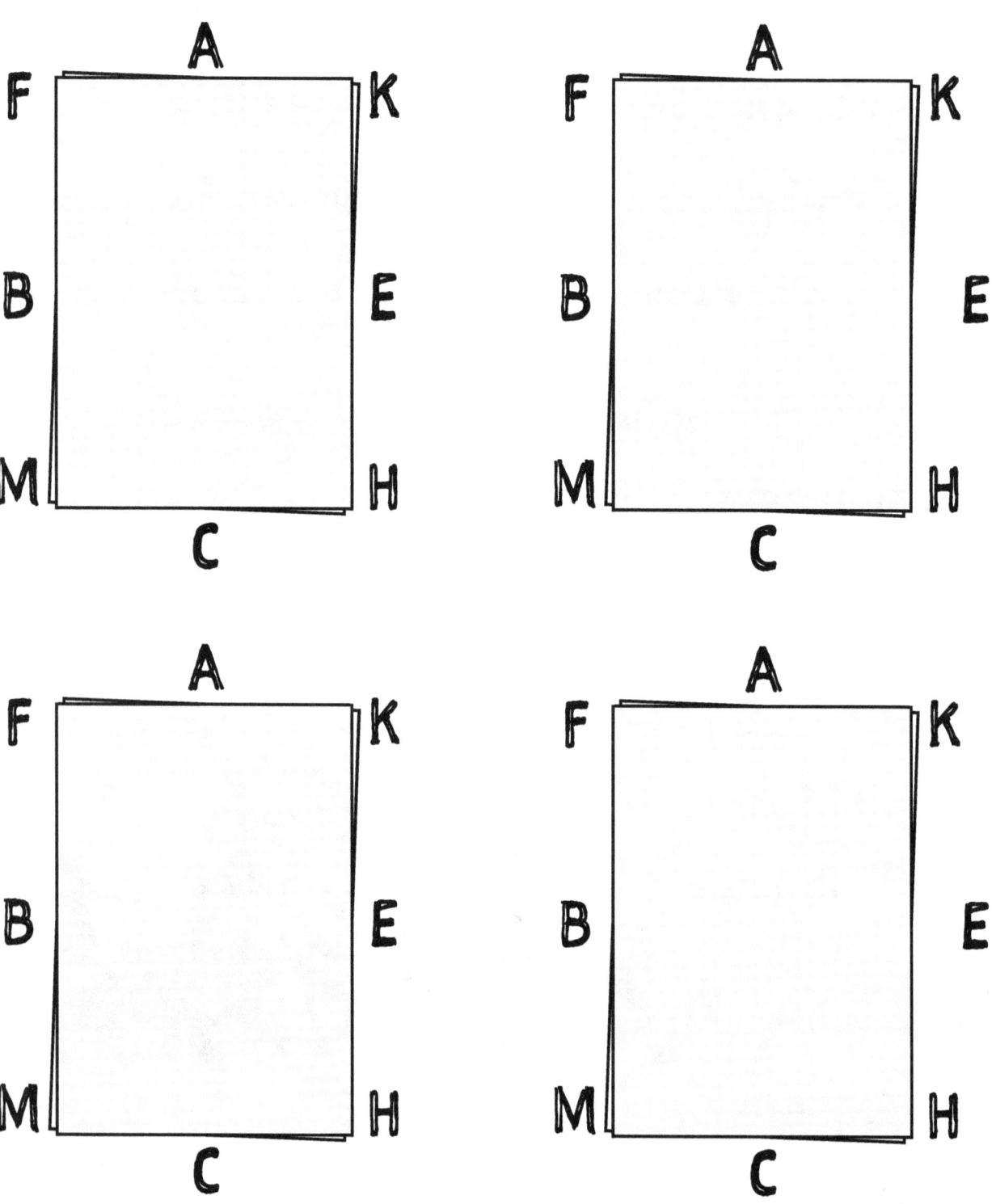

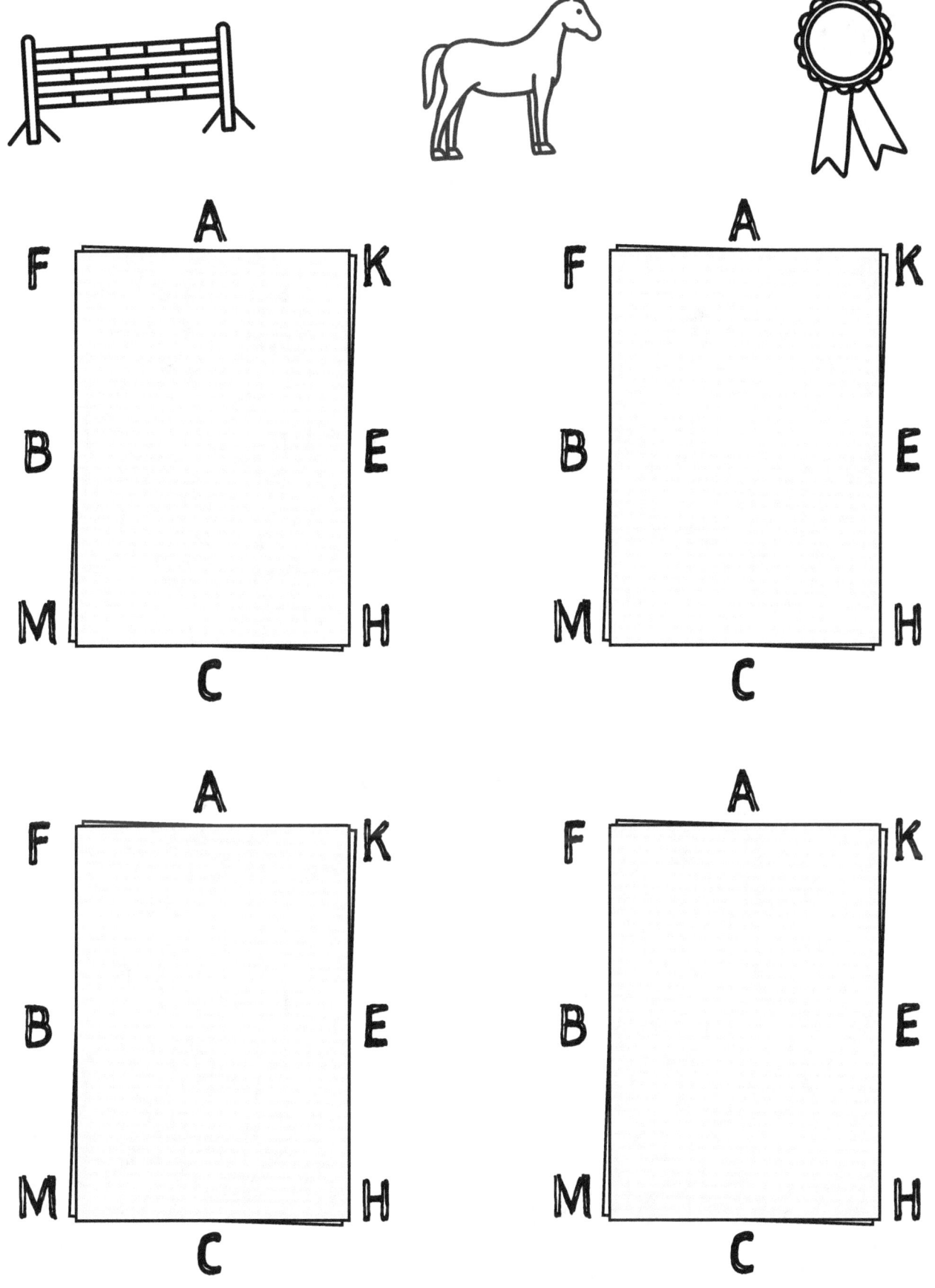

FOOTFALL

Can you colour in the correct sequence of footfalls? The starting point has been done for you.

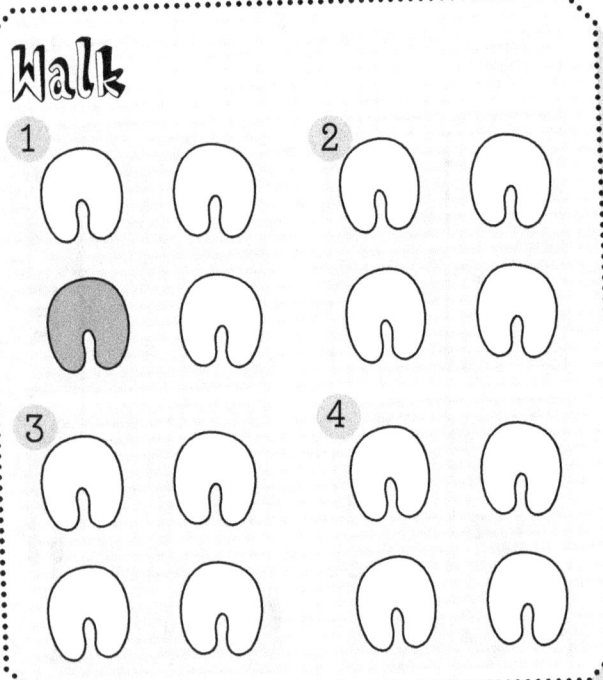

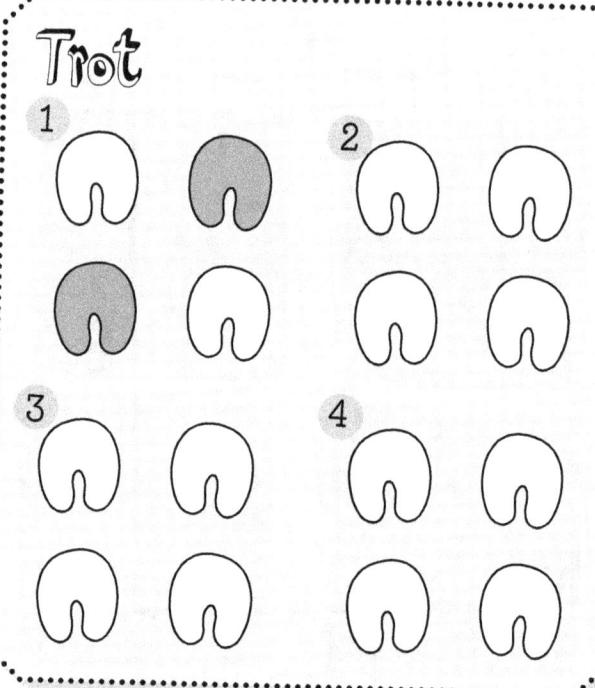

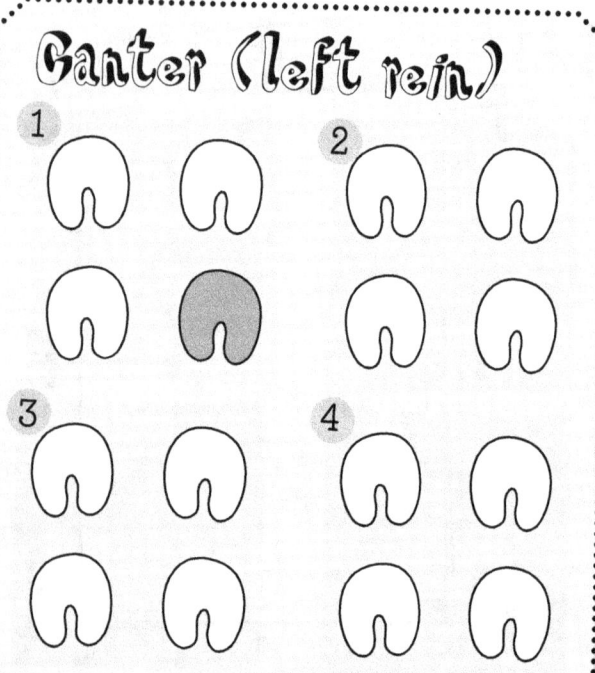

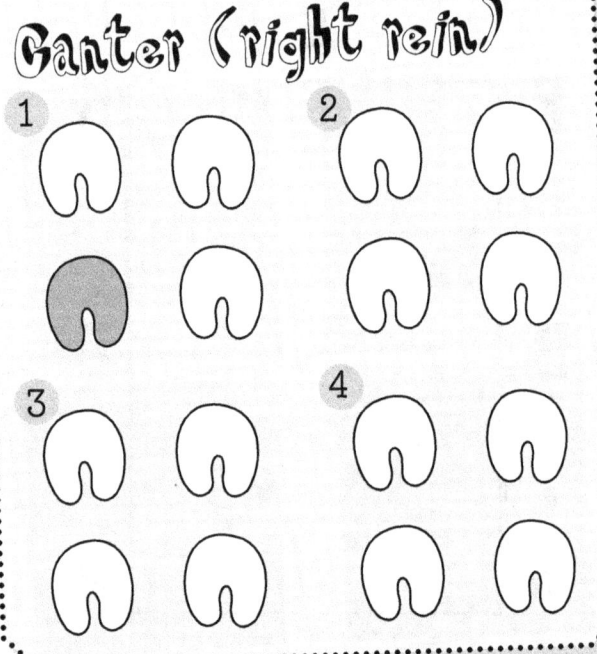

Answers on page 172

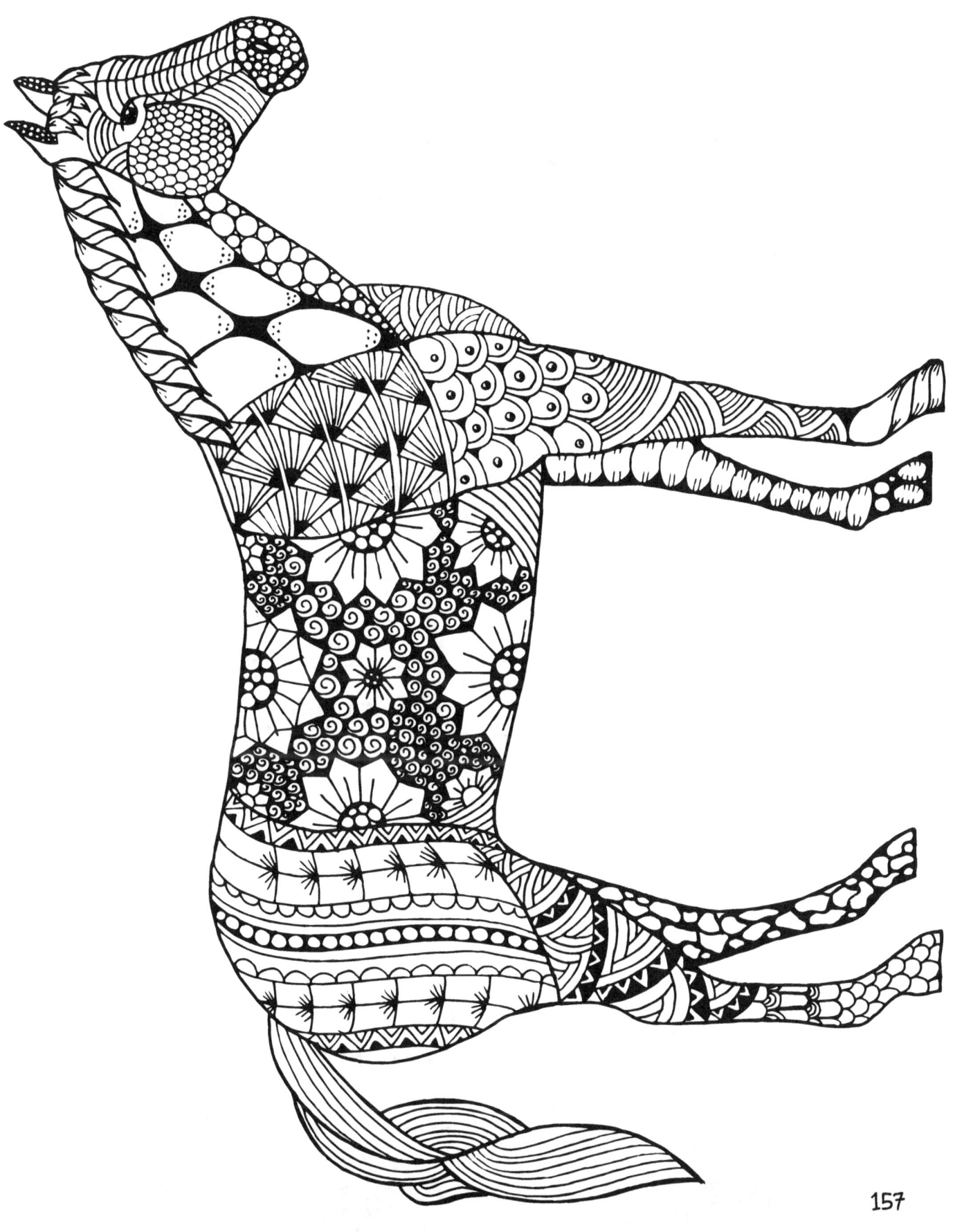

MONTH: ....

My riding goals

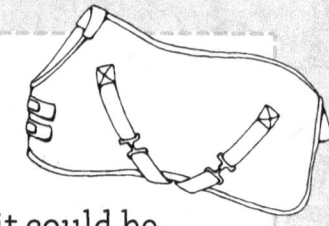

What would you like to do better or learn? For example, it could be to keep your heels down, develop a deeper seat, master the half halt, improve your jumping, ride a perfect leg yield, or maybe even try a *piaffe*.

Make a list of the things you want to focus on this month. If you're not sure what to pick, ask your instructor.

Goal 1: _____
_____
_____

Goal 2: _____
_____
_____

Goal 3: _____
_____
_____

I .... do hereby commit to practising these things every time I ride.

Signed: ....
Date: ....

158

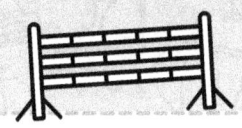

Using a goal tracker can help you achieve your targets.

GOAL	Colour in a horseshoe every time you practise
1	
2	
3	

Write or draw your goals!

WEEK ONE

What went well:

* _____
* _____
* _____
* _____
* _____

What I need to practise:

1. _____
2. _____
3. _____

Pony of the week

THIS WEEK I HAVE ...

- ○ Groomed
- ○ Cleaned tack
- ○ Mucked out
- ○ Had a lesson
- ○ Helped with feeding
- ○ Been for a hack
- ○ Learnt something new
- ○ Ridden a different pony

MY LESSON TRACKER

Name: _____

Age: _____

○ Mare

○ Gelding

Q: What type of phone do horses like best?
A: Apple!

WEEK TWO

What went well:

* _____
* _____
* _____
* _____
* _____

What I need to practise:

1. _____

2. _____

3. _____

Pony of the week

THIS WEEK I HAVE ...

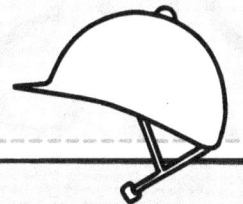

- ○ Groomed
- ○ Cleaned tack
- ○ Mucked out
- ○ Had a lesson
- ○ Helped with feeding
- ○ Been for a hack
- ○ Learnt something new
- ○ Ridden a different pony

MY LESSON TRACKER

Name: _____

Age: _____

- ○ Mare
- ○ Gelding

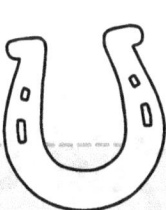

WEEK THREE

What went well:

* _____
* _____
* _____
* _____
* _____

What I need to practise:

1. _____

2. _____

3. _____

Pony of the week

THIS WEEK I HAVE ...

- ◯ Groomed
- ◯ Cleaned tack
- ◯ Mucked out
- ◯ Had a lesson
- ◯ Helped with feeding
- ◯ Been for a hack
- ◯ Learnt something new
- ◯ Ridden a different pony

MY LESSON TRACKER

Name: _____

Age: _____

◯ Mare

◯ Gelding

Did you know?

In New Jersey, it is illegal to drive a horse attached to a sleigh or sled on a highway unless there are bells attached to the harness.

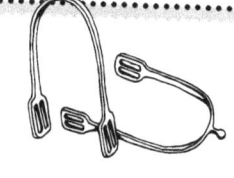

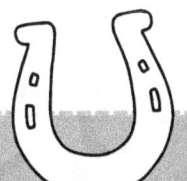

WEEK FOUR

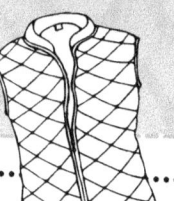

What went well:

* _____
* _____
* _____
* _____
* _____

What I need to practise:

1. _____
   _____

2. _____
   _____

3. _____

Pony of the week

THIS WEEK I HAVE ...

- ○ Groomed
- ○ Cleaned tack
- ○ Mucked out
- ○ Had a lesson
- ○ Helped with feeding
- ○ Been for a hack
- ○ Learnt something new
- ○ Ridden a different pony

MY LESSON TRACKER

Name: _____

Age: _____

- ○ Mare
- ○ Gelding

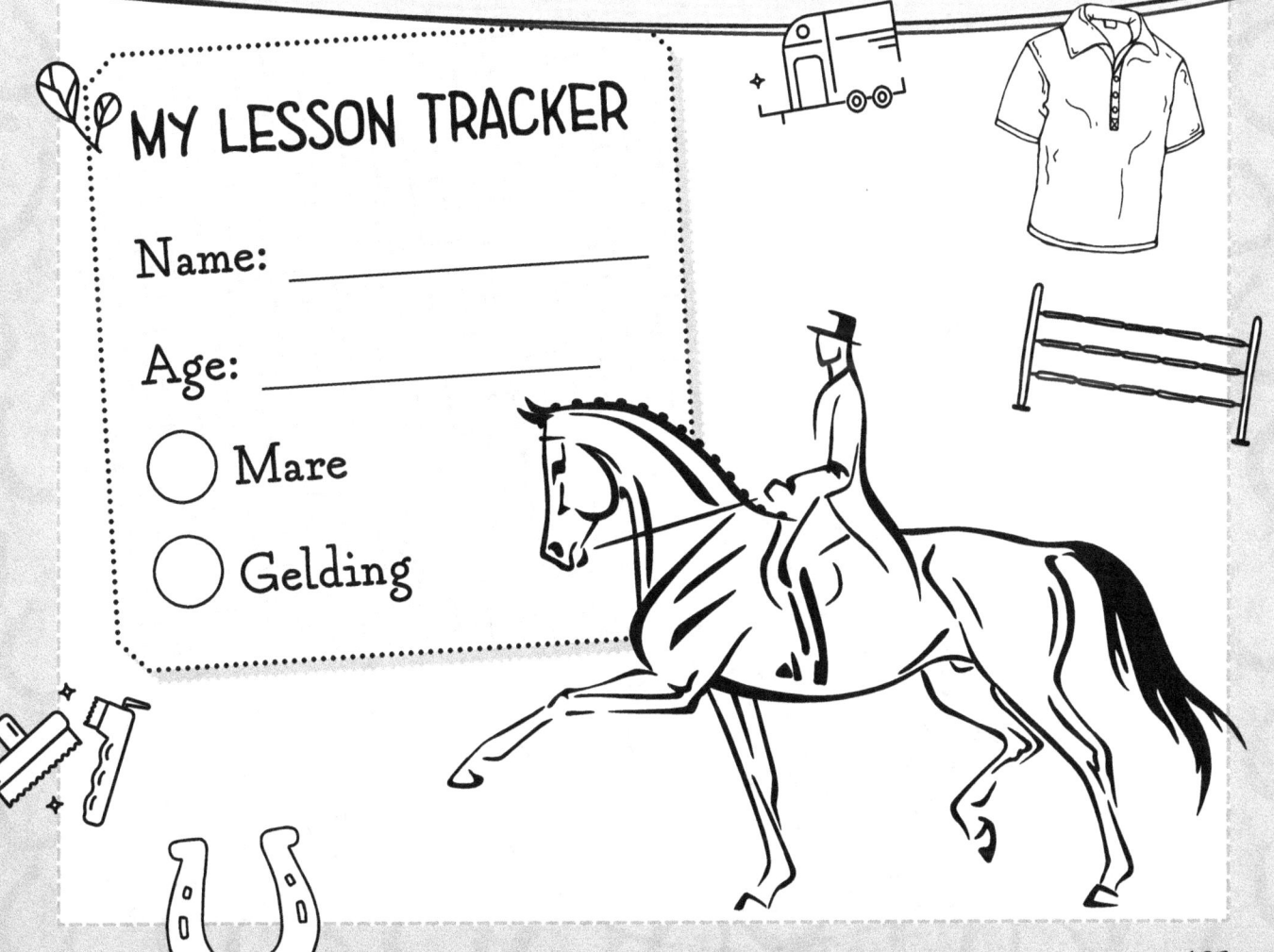

Rosette tangle

Can you help the rider to collect the rosette?

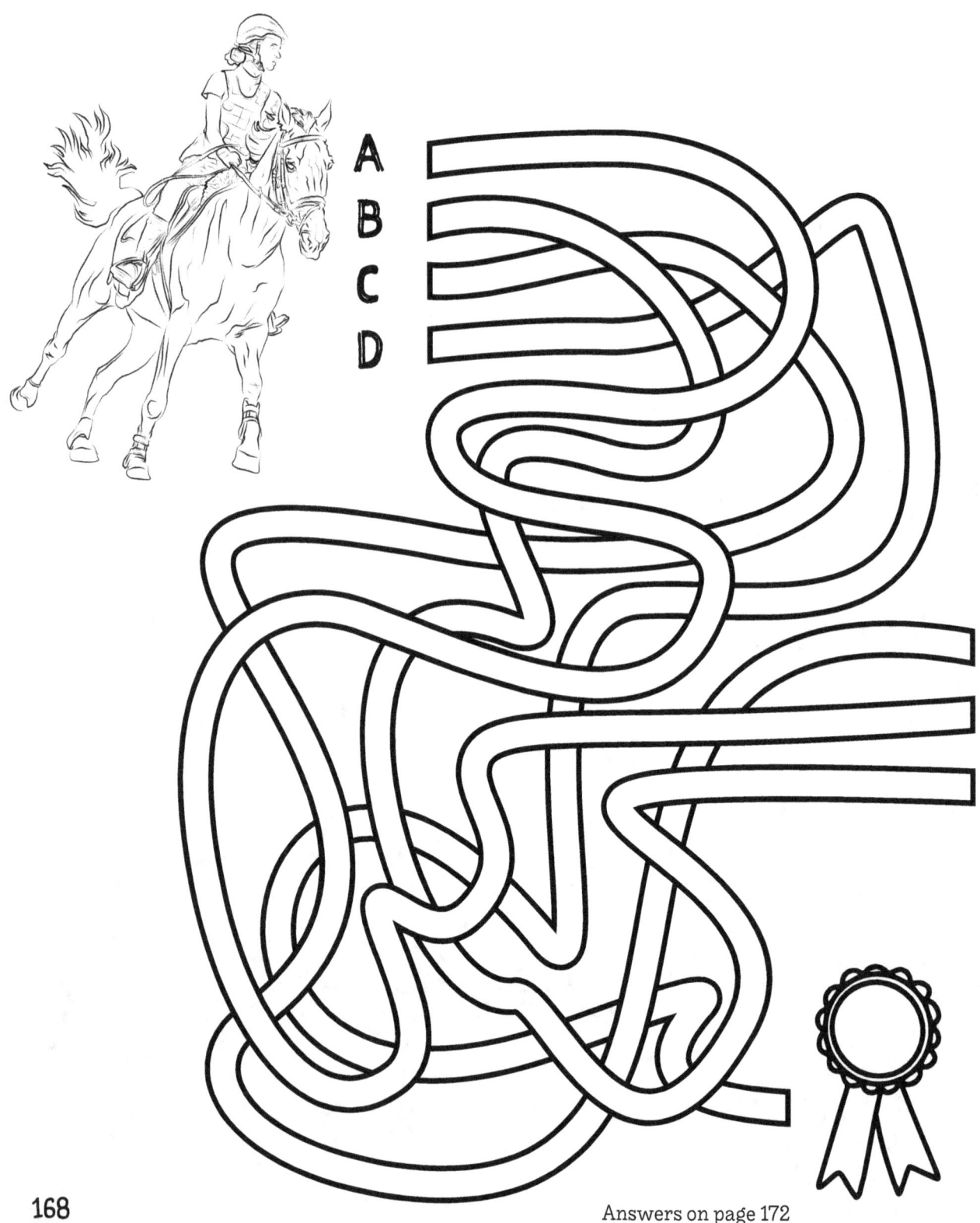

HORSE BOOKS I HAVE READ

It could be fiction or non-fiction. Don't forget about the knights of old, modern war horses and brave police horses. And stories about unicorns and centaurs count too!

Title	Author	My review	Carrot rating 1 = did not finish 5 = brilliant
			🥕🥕🥕🥕🥕
			🥕🥕🥕🥕🥕
			🥕🥕🥕🥕🥕
			🥕🥕🥕🥕🥕
			🥕🥕🥕🥕🥕
			🥕🥕🥕🥕🥕
			🥕🥕🥕🥕🥕
			🥕🥕🥕🥕🥕
			🥕🥕🥕🥕🥕
			🥕🥕🥕🥕🥕

Title	Author	My review	Carrot rating 1 = did not finish 5 = brilliant
			🥕🥕🥕🥕🥕
			🥕🥕🥕🥕🥕
			🥕🥕🥕🥕🥕
			🥕🥕🥕🥕🥕
			🥕🥕🥕🥕🥕
			🥕🥕🥕🥕🥕
			🥕🥕🥕🥕🥕
			🥕🥕🥕🥕🥕
			🥕🥕🥕🥕🥕
			🥕🥕🥕🥕🥕
			🥕🥕🥕🥕🥕
			🥕🥕🥕🥕🥕

ANSWERS

Page 14: Tack Up

Page 16: Horse Breed Anagrams
SHETLAND
ARABIAN
MUSTANG
SHIRE
FJORD
LUSITANO
PERCHERON
MORGAN
HALFINGER
APPALOOSA
FRIESIAN

Page 28: Name That Clip
A. Trace
B. Strip
C. Blanket
D. Chaser
E. Full
F. Irish
G. Bib
H. Hunter

Page 70: Hungry As A Horse

Page 86: Label The Points Of A Horse

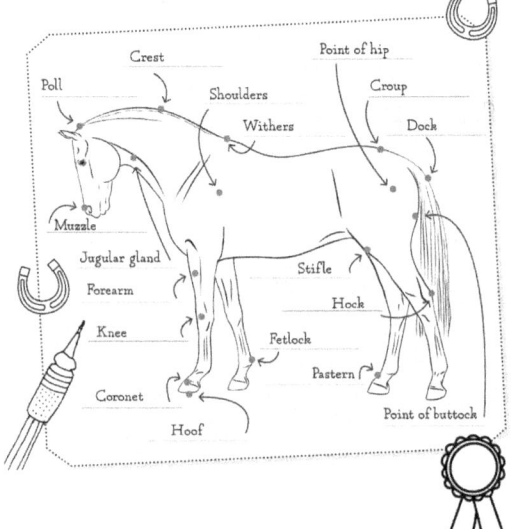

Page 100: Amazing Maze

Pages 154-155: Change Of Rein

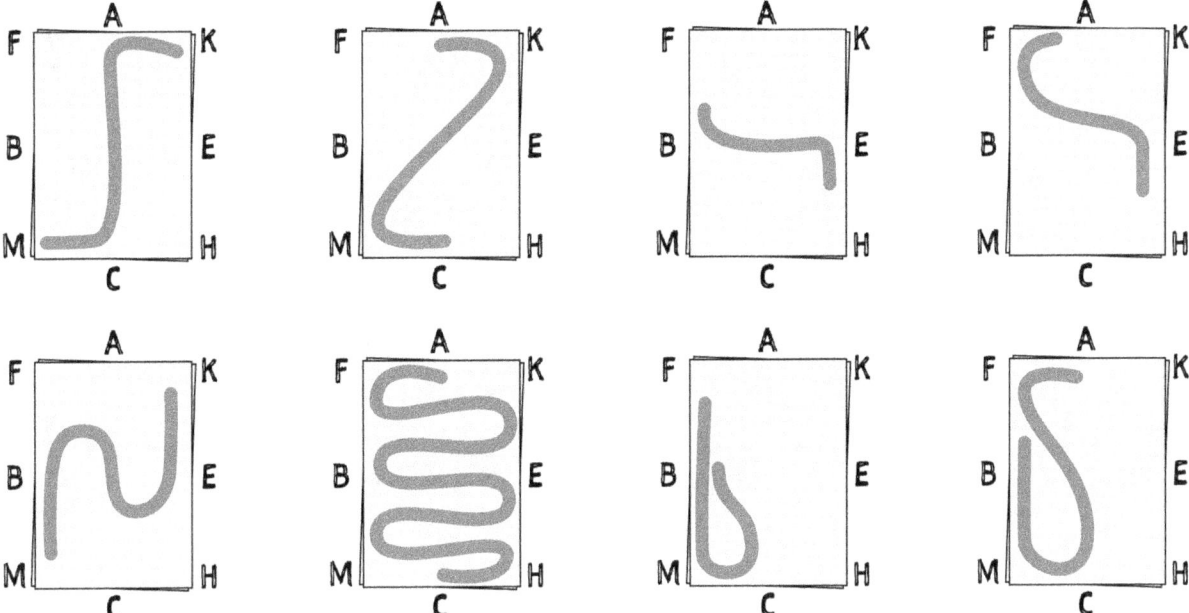

Don't forget, these can all be reversed so there are lots of options.

Page 156: Footfall

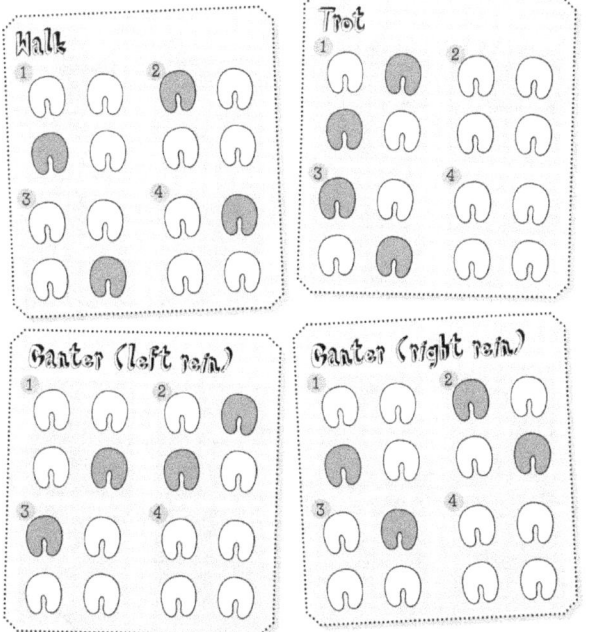

Page 168: Rosette Tangle

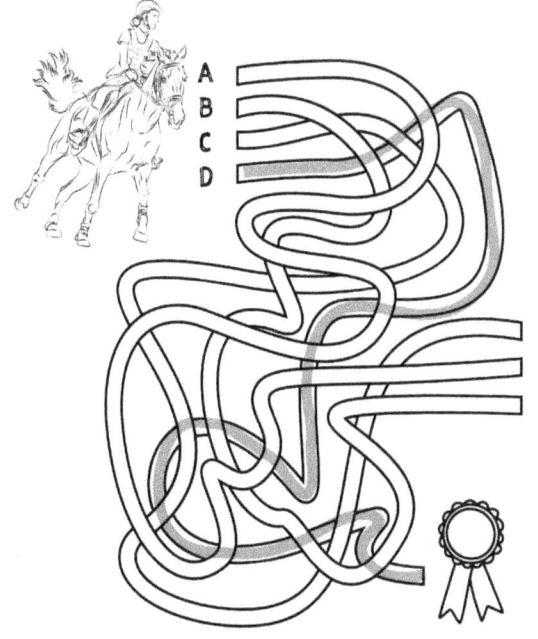

MY NOTES

MY NOTES

MY NOTES

MY NOTES

MY NOTES

MY NOTES

www.ingramcontent.com/pod-product-compliance
Lightning Source LLC
Chambersburg PA
CBHW081708100526
44590CB00022B/3705